Innovative Reporting in
Foreign Currency Translation

Research for Business Decisions, No. 85

Richard N. Farmer, Series Editor

Professor of International Business
Indiana University

Other Titles in This Series

Innovative Reporting in
Foreign Currency Translation

by
Denise M. Guithues

UMI RESEARCH PRESS
Ann Arbor, Michigan

Produced and distributed by
UMI Research Press
an imprint of
University Microfilms International
A Xerox Information Resources Company
Ann Arbor, Michigan 48106

Library of Congress Cataloging in Publication Data

Guithues, Denise M.
  Innovative reporting in foreign currency translation.

  (Research for business decisions ; no. 85)
  Revision of thesis (Ph.D.)—Saint Louis University,
1983.
  Bibliography: p.
  Includes index.
  1. Foreign exchange—Accounting. 2. Financial
statement. I. Title. II. Series.
  HG3853.7.G85 1986   657'.48   85-22757
  ISBN 0-8357-1720-8 (alk. paper)

*To my family, who have provided me
with constant support and encouragement*

Contents

List of Figures

List of Tables

Acknowledgments

I would like to thank Dr. Elwood Miller, Dr. Donald Tyree, and Dr. Charles Wuller of St. Louis University for their assistance in the completion of this book. Thanks also to Florence Guithues for her assistance in the typing of the original version of the manuscript. Special thanks must go to my parents, Dr. and Mrs. Henry J. Guithues, who instilled in me the desire to learn and the determination to work toward my goals. To them I owe a debt I can never repay.

1

Introduction

The purpose of this book is to present empirical evidence on the current state of financial reporting disclosures on foreign currency translation and to offer suggestions for the improvement of these disclosures. This chapter will introduce the problems to be examined and the research methodology to be employed.

Statement of the Problem

As the number and size of multinational corporations increase, financial administrators are faced with the problem of consolidating the results of their foreign and domestic operations in a manner that will produce meaningful consolidated financial information. This task is complicated by the fact that the financial records of a company's foreign and domestic operations are maintained in different currencies whose interrelationships are constantly changing as a result of the floating foreign-exchange-rate system. The lack of a stable basis of translation leads to a number of problems, some of which are similar to the problems created by changing price-levels. These problems, which will be discussed more fully in later chapters, run the gamut from the question of the appropriate exchange rate to use in each case to the question of what the translated results are actually communicating to the statement user. The desire to achieve more meaningful consolidated financial reporting led the Financial Accounting Standards Board (FASB) to address the issue of foreign currency translation in several official pronouncements.

The most recent of these pronouncements was FASB *Statement No. 52*, "Foreign Currency Translation," which was issued in December 1981. This statement was reactionary and intended to solve problems — such as violent swings in reported earnings and distortions of financial statement relationships — which had proliferated in the area of foreign currency translation under the guidelines offered by its October 1975 predecessor, FASB *Statement No. 8*, "Accounting for the Translation of Foreign Currency

Transactions and Foreign Currency Financial Statements." As a result, instead of building a new, structurally sound, foundation, *Statement No. 52* merely repaired the cracks in an unsound substructure. This repair job cannot be expected to last. *Statement No. 52* should have developed more flexible guidelines for foreign currency translation. Such guidelines would have been in accordance with the objectives of financial reporting delineated in FASB *Statement of Financial Accounting Concepts No. 1*, "Objectives of Financial Reporting by Business Enterprises." While it is true that the objectives outlined in *Statement No. 52* do correlate with those objectives set forth in *Concept No. 1*, it is the opinion of this author that *Statement No. 52* does not fully accomplish its objectives.

We will examine those areas of FASB *Statement No. 52* which are considered to be deficient. We will then propose some possible guidelines for foreign currency translation that could fulfill the objectives of financial reporting more completely than those guidelines currently in existence.

Review of FASB Statement No. 52

Statement No. 52 takes a functional currency approach to foreign currency translation. As a result, it requires that the first step in the translation process be the determination of the functional currency, which is defined as the currency of the primary economic environment in which the entity operates. This means that, depending on the circumstances, the functional currency could be (1) the reporting currency (such as the United States dollar), (2) the currency of record (usually a foreign currency), or (3) a third currency in which the company conducts operations. (Functional currencies will be discussed more fully in chapter 3.) Then, based on the functional currency, the translation method is selected. If the reporting currency is deemed to be the functional currency, the temporal method of translation will be used. (The temporal method was the method of translation required by *Statement No. 8*. It will be explained later in this chapter.) On the other hand, if the foreign currency is also the functional currency, the current rate method of translation will generally be used. (This method of translation will also be explained later in the chapter.)

An exception to the latter rule occurs when the foreign entity is operating in a highly inflationary environment. In such a case, the financial statements of the foreign operation will be remeasured using the temporal method of translation, regardless of which currency is determined to be the functional currency. For the purpose of this rule, the FASB defined a highly inflationary environment to be one that has experienced a three-year cumulative inflation rate of 100 percent or more. As mentioned previously, this highly complex area has been further complicated by fluctuating exchange rates which have resulted in violent swings in earnings known as the "yo-yo" effect.

The net result of these options and uncontrollable variables makes it highly unlikely that a multinational company will be able to translate the statements of its foreign operations without some degree of distortion. Faced with this situation, there is a need for some method of informative disclosure which will minimize the distorting effects of foreign currency translation on financial information. This will allow for a more meaningful presentation. As of this date, no such informative disclosure model exists. The objective of this research will be to examine the current methods of disclosure with the primary goal of developing an informative disclosure model that will significantly improve the quality of financial reporting by multinational companies.

Approach to a Reasoned Solution

The first step in this analysis will be a discussion of the nature of exchange rates, the purpose for which they are intended, the factors that enter into their determination, and their efficiency as a translation mechanism. This will be followed by a review of the background of foreign currency translation and the international operation environment, including general summaries of *Statement No. 8* and *Statement No. 52*. Such a review seems necessary since the nature and cause of a change should be considered prior to recommending (or examining) how the economic effects of a change should be reported.

The next step will be a review of the related literature along with a critical analysis of the statements. This review will include examinations of (1) the provisions of the statements; (2) the accounting issues and tax aspects involved; (3) the effects on multinational corporations in general and on the financial results of specific multinational corporations; (4) the impacts on financial statement analysis, managing and controlling the accounting and/or economic risk of exchange rate changes; and (5) the conceptual issues underlying foreign currency accounting and reporting.

The above reviews will be complemented by an empirical investigation which will consist of an analysis of the 1981 annual reports of the 100 largest United States multinational corporations as delineated in the July 5, 1982 issue of *Forbes*. Each of these annual reports will be analyzed to ascertain the method and scope of foreign currency translation disclosure practices. The twin objectives of this research will be (a) to document the deficiencies that exist in the current methods of reporting the effects of foreign currency translation, and (b) to develop an informative disclosure model – using a matrix approach supported by management discussion –

that will significantly improve the availability and usefulness of foreign currency translation information so that the financial statement user will be able to draw more meaningful conclusions from the information that is presented.

Summary

Foreign currency translation has assumed critical importance. Not only has international business activity increased through growth in foreign trade and proliferation of subsidiaries of multinational corporations, both in number and in size, but the international economic environments have also become more volatile. Global inflation has taken on major proportions, resulting in erratic changes in the purchasing powers of different currencies — their real values. In addition, the so-called "system" of floating exchange rates has created erratic prices of currencies — their market values. Both phenomena have exacerbated the problems of foreign currency translation.

To date, the systems suggested for coping with these problems have followed a pattern of crisis management — attempting to solve problems after they have reached critical stages. Furthermore, standard-setters seem to have been predisposed to seek out and apply normative (standardized) methods to dissimilar situations. Consequently, when statement issuers presented the required information, it either conflicted with economic sense or encouraged uneconomic actions. Neither is a desirable product of accounting information. What is needed is a systems approach that analyzes the problems (general and specific) and then suggests realistic measures which provide useful information to financial statement users given the particular circumstances.

The need for useful information was recognized by the FASB in *Statement of Financial Accounting Concepts No. 1,* "Objectives of Financial Reporting by Business Enterprises." In broad terms, the objectives called for the presentation of information that was "useful to present and potential investors and creditors and other users in making rational investment, credit, and similar decisions. The information should be comprehensible to those who have a reasonable understanding of business and economic activities and are willing to study the information with reasonable diligence."[1] In narrower terms, *SFA Concepts No. 1* stated:

> Financial reporting should provide information to help present and potential investors and creditors and other users in assessing the amounts, timing, and uncertainty of prospective cash receipts from dividends or interest and the proceeds from the sale, redemption, or maturity of securities or loans. The prospects for those cash receipts are affected by an enterprise's ability to generate enough cash to meet its obligations when

due and its other cash operating needs, to reinvest in operations, and to pay cash dividends and may also be affected by perceptions of investors and creditors generally about that ability, which affect market prices of the enterprise's securities. Thus, financial reporting should provide information to help investors, creditors, and others assess the amounts, timing, and uncertainty of prospective net cash inflows to the related enterprise.[2]

SFA Concepts No. 1 also stipulated that:

> Financial reporting should provide information about the economic resources of an enterprise, the claims to those resources (obligations of the enterprise to transfer resources to other entities and owners' equity), and the effects of transactions, events and circumstances that change resources and claims to those resources.[3]

Most importantly, this statement specified that "Financial reporting should include explanations and interpretations to help users understand the financial information provided."[4]

In addition it should be pointed out that *SFA Concepts No. 1* called for prospective as well as historical information, called for information that made economic sense, and effectively required disaggregated data (as well as consolidated) if the information was to be useful to users, such as creditors.

We will examine the nature of exchange rates in the next chapter, because it is difficult to account for or report on something unless that something is understood. In order to achieve an understanding of foreign currency translation, one must achieve an understanding of the translation mechanism currently in use — exchange rates. After the nature of exchange rates has been examined, the area of foreign currency translation will be analyzed.

2

Exchange Rates

Introduction

The international business environment is one in which there is no universal medium of exchange. As a result, when transactions are denominated in foreign currencies two basic needs arise. First, there is the need for translation. That is, the transaction which is stated in terms of a foreign currency must be re-expressed or restated in terms of the local currency before it can be recorded in the local accounting records. Second, settlement of the transaction requires conversion. This means that when payment is due, a sufficient amount of the local currency must be exchanged for the stated amount of foreign currency so that payment can be made.

At present, both translation and conversion of foreign currency involve the use of exchange rates. Therefore, in order to gain a more thorough understanding of foreign currency translation, it is important to examine the nature of exchange rates. The questions which will be discussed here include: What is an exchange rate and what is its intended purpose? What determines an exchange rate? Do exchange rates provide the most efficient translation mechanism, or is there something preferable to them?

Answers to the above questions should provide a useful foundation upon which to assess the relative merits of the various translation methods which exist or have been suggested.

Definitions

An exchange rate has been defined as a "relative price of two national monies."[1] More specifically, it can be stated that the exchange rate is "the ratio between a unit of one currency and the amount of another currency for which that unit can be exchanged at a particular time."[2] As such, it can be seen that exchange rates are designed to facilitate the actual exchange of one currency for another. It would appear that exchange rates are relatively straightforward. However, this is unfortunately not the case.

Exchange rates are normally quoted in terms of a buying rate, a flat rate, and a selling rate. The buying rate is that which a bank will pay for a foreign currency, the selling rate is the rate a bank will charge for the currency, and the flat rate is an average of the buying and selling rates. In addition, the exchange rate which is quoted will often depend on various factors such as the market sector and type of foreign-exchange instrument involved. The foreign-exchange market can be divided into four main sectors: (1) retail—dealings with the general public; (2) wholesale—tradings among banking institutions and, where permitted, between large firms and brokers; (3) foreign—dealings between domestic and foreign banks; and (4) supranational—dealings among large multinational corporations and large private banks. The basic types of foreign-exchange instruments include foreign currencies, bank transfers, bills of exchange, letters of credit, and forward exchange contracts.[3]

These varied circumstances call for different exchange rates, which can usually be classified into three main categories: spot rates, forward rates, and differential rates. Spot rates are the rates quoted for immediate delivery of a currency (usually two days). Forward rates are those quoted for delivery of a currency at a specified future date (usually within one year, but after the period for the spot rate). Differential rates may be either preferential or penalty rates which are limited to special markets or customers. They are normally found in economies where the government controls foreign exchange and differ from the spot and forward rates. In such cases, the government will often establish exchange rates based on the status of the transaction involved. If the government considers a transaction to be economically favorable, the exchange rates attached to it will often reflect that fact. That is, the government will often establish more favorable exchange rates for those transactions that it wishes to encourage. On the other hand, the government will also establish less favorable exchange rates for those transactions that it wishes to discourage. "Where controlled rates differ widely from the free-market rate for a currency, black-market rates usually appear as an equalizing mechanism. Consequently, the mere existence of a black-market rate is evidence of an overvalued currency."[4]

Historical Determinants of Exchange Rates

Answering the question of what determines an exchange rate is by no means a simple task. This is because there are no clear-cut relationships on which to rely. The best that one can do is to examine some of the factors that play a part in this determination. The first step in this examination will address some of the underlying theory of exchange rates. This will be followed by a more detailed analysis of some of the factors involved in exchange rate determination.

In modern times, the operative system of exchange rates has evolved from a gold bullion standard to a system of floating exchange rates with several alternative systems used in between.

The "gold bullion standard prevailed from about 1870 until 1914, and intermittently thereafter until 1944."[5] Under this system, central governments defined their currencies in terms of a specific amount of gold bullion and agreed to redeem their currencies at the set rates (mint parities). However, as a commodity, the international market price of a currency (the exchange rate) would fluctuate above or below parity based on the supply and demand of that currency relative to others. "If excessive demand forced the market price of a currency above the parity band, external debtors found it cheaper to pay their debts in gold. Conversely, if insufficient demand for a currency lowered its market price below the parity band, external creditors demanded payments in gold."[6] Under this system, unless a country maintained a reasonable trade balance over time, continuing trade deficits would drain its gold reserves. The lower level of gold reserves would, in turn, result in a shrinkage of that country's money supply and a lower internal price level. Lower domestic prices would eventually make the country's products more competitive in the international marketplace. As exports increased, the demand for the country's currency would also increase resulting in an inflow of gold reserves. With a self-balancing system such as this, the governments' role was a passive one in which they would merely permit the free flow of gold to stabilize economies and exchange rates. Thus, the gold bullion standard acted as an automatic stabilizer, at least in theory.

Unfortunately, there were inherent problems with the gold bullion standard, which eventually caused it to be abandoned. These problems stemmed mainly from several invalid assumptions upon which the system was based:

1. The worldwide gold supply would increase yearly in the same proportion as the net growth in the supply of goods and services and in the proper locations.

2. Each country's available gold supply would be such that trade imbalances would bring about the necessary changes in its money supply and price level in a reasonably short time.

3. International trade and competition would be free of all artificial restrictions.

4. Scare outflows of gold (through causes such as fears of political instabilities) would not occur.[7]

In addition, governments generally preferred to take a more active role, especially in matters influencing their internal economies.

In 1944, following World War II, the United States and most of its allies ratified the Bretton Woods Agreement which set up an adjustable-parity exchange-rate system under which exchange rates were fixed (pegged) within narrow intervention limits (pegs) by the United States and foreign central banks buying and selling foreign currencies. This agreement, fostered by a new spirit of international cooperation, was in response to the financial chaos that had reigned before and during the war.

In addition to setting up fixed exchange parities (par values) of currencies in relationship to gold, the agreement established the International Monetary Fund (IMF) to act as the "custodian" of the system. Under the system, member governments were obligated to defend the exchange rates within a narrow band of about 1 percent above or below parity (the official exchange rate). The revaluation or devaluation of a currency was called for only in the case of "fundamental disequilibria" (chronic surpluses or deficits in a nation's balance of payments). Despite the fact that the IMF expressed currencies in terms of gold, in practice currencies were expressed in terms of dollars, and the Bretton Woods Agreement became a rigid dollar standard. This situation arose because the United States was the only country that agreed to redeem its currency for gold.

Naturally, the dollar could not serve as both a national and an international currency, since under these conditions international liquidity (total trade financing potential) could be expanded only through larger balance-of-payments deficits on the part of the United States. The ensuing massive United States balance-of-payments deficits led to an erosion of confidence in the dollar as a store of wealth, the cancellation of the gold convertibility of the dollar in August 1971 by the United States, and the signing of the Smithsonian Agreement in December 1971 by the major trading nations, referred to as The Group of Ten. This was an attempt to restore monetary order by devaluing the dollar and establishing a wider parity band (plus or minus 2.25 percent). Despite this effort, the United States continued to experience balance-of-payments deficits. In early 1973, an additional 10 percent devaluation of the dollar, along with agreement of several European Economic Community (EEC) member nations to let their currencies float against the dollar, dealt the death knell to the Bretton Woods and Smithsonian Agreements.

Allowing exchange rates to float in the midst of financial chaos was like setting a boat adrift in the middle of a storm — smooth sailing was next to impossible. To make matters worse, the tripling of oil prices by the Organization of Petroleum Exporting Countries (OPEC) during 1973 hit the foreign exchange markets like a hurricane, causing global inflation to rise with the tide. However, the circumstances under which floating exchange rates were introduced are by no means the only problem with the system. The lack of an official common denominator and the diminished authority of the IMF have not helped matters. Money has become a commodity that is bought and sold at market prices. In the international economic sense, money has become a circular concept — defined only in terms of the price that each currency will bring in other currencies.[8]

In addition, three important trends developed that contributed to the problem.

> First, there was a persistent increase in liquid resources available to the private sector relative to the monetary reserves held by the central banks. (The money supply was no longer tied to a country's gold reserves and the multiplier effect allowed for this growth.) Second, there were constantly improving techniques permitting market participants to shift large amounts of capital rapidly from one currency to another. Third, there were improving communication methods making information available instantaneously to a growing number of analysts throughout the world.[9]

Contemporary Impacts upon Rates

As a result, the "main theme of the modern view of exchange-rate determination emphasizes that the exchange rate, being a relative price of two national monies, is determined primarily by the relative supplies and demands for these monies."[10] Four of the main reasons for holding money arc: (1) for the purpose of conducting transactions, (2) for the purpose of speculating, (3) for the purpose of saving and earning a return, and (4) for precautionary purposes. On the other hand, the main determinants of the money supply are government policies and actions, which can take many forms. Planned transactions can also affect exchange rates by affecting the demand and supply of different currencies. If a United States company plans to purchase goods from a Japanese company which requires payment in yen, the United States company's demand for yen will increase. All these items "will, over time, affect the supply of and demand for currencies,"[11] thereby, affecting the exchange rates.

According to John E. Rule, it is the views of participants in the foreign-exchange markets that "give rise to the buying and selling pressures on currencies on a day to day basis."[12] The views of these participants, such as traders, bankers, and businessmen, are in turn influenced by political, economic and psychological factors.

Political Factors

The political factors influencing exchange rates include the established monetary policy along with government action or inaction on items such as the money supply, inflation, taxes, and deficit financing. Active government intervention or manipulation, such as central bank activity in the foreign currency markets, also have an impact. Other political factors influencing exchange rates include the political stability of a country and its relative economic exposure (the perceived need for certain levels and types of imports). Finally, there is also the influence of the International Monetary Fund.

Economic Factors

Economic factors affecting exchange rates include hedging activities, interest rates, inflationary pressures, trade imbalances, and Euromarket activities.

Irving Fisher, an American economist, developed a theory relating exchange rates to interest rates. This proposition, known as the Fisher Effect, "states that interest rate differentials tend to reflect exchange rate expectations."[13]

On the other hand, the purchasing-power-parity theory relates exchange rates to inflationary pressures. In its absolute version, this theory "states that the equilibrium exchange rate equals the ratio of domestic to foreign prices. The relative version of the theory relates changes in the exchange rate to changes in price ratios."[14]

In an article on international money management appearing in *Business Week*, it was observed that "the gyrations of the currency markets are now dominated mainly by shifts of capital—meaning shifts of stateless money in the Euromarkets. These movements are forcing exchange rates up and down beyond anything justified by accepted economic criteria."[15]

Other economic factors influencing exchange rates are included in a theory proposed by Dornbush, who presented both a long-run view and a short-run view of exchange rate determinants. According to Dornbush, the long-run determinants of exchange rates are "the nominal quantities of monies, the real money demands and the relative price structure."[16] Among the factors that exert an influence on real money demand are "interest rates, expected inflation, and real income growth."[17] In the short run, Dornbush states that exchange rates are determined by "interest arbitrage together with speculation about future spot rates."[18]

Psychological Factors

Psychological factors also influence exchange rates. These factors include market anticipation, speculative pressures, and future expectations. In fact, Frenkel and Musa both emphasize the role of expectations when discussing the determinants of exchange rates.[19]

Suitability for Use in Foreign Currency Translations

In the final analysis, exchange rates are designed to facilitate the exchange of one currency for another. Accordingly, exchange rates represent reasonable mechanisms with which to translate foreign-currency *transactions*, particularly those that will be settled in the short term. "Attaching more relevance than this to exchange rates and using them as surrogate measures to evaluate past performances or future economic decisions can only be done at great risk."[20] Therefore, another tool such as purchasing-power-parity indexes should be found for use in the translation of foreign currency. However, at present, such a tool is not available. Until such an index does become generally available, the use of exchange rates in the translation of foreign currency must suffice. Thus, measures should be taken to alert users of the information to the inherent deficiencies resulting from the use of exchange rates. This could be done in part through the use of supplemental explanatory information.

3

History of Foreign Currency Translation

General Background

Current translation theory is tied directly to the consolidation theory expressed in August 1959 in *Accounting Research Bulletin No. 51*, "Consolidated Financial Statements." The influence of *ARB No. 51* can be seen in FASB *Statement No. 52*, which states:

> Financial statements are intended to present information in financial terms about the performance, financial position and cash flows of an enterprise. For this purpose, the financial statements of separate entities within an enterprise, which may exist and operate in different economic and currency environments, are consolidated and presented as though they were the financial statements of a single enterprise.[1]

Prior to the adoption of FASB *Statement No. 8*, existing accounting pronouncements in the area of foreign currency translation dealt solely with translating foreign financial statements and not with foreign currency transactions. Under these guidelines, companies could select from several acceptable alternatives to account for foreign currency transactions and to translate foreign currency financial statements of subsidiaries and branches. With the adoption of *Statement No. 8*, the situation changed.

Historical Background

Foreign currency translation is an area with a long and colorful history. Its origins date back to the beginnings of trade between individuals using different monies. Early evidence of the need for translation of transactions can be found in the *Summa De Arithmetica, Geometria, Proportioni et Proportionalita*, published by Luca Pacioli during the fifteenth century. This publication was mainly a treatise on mathematics, but it included a section describing a system of double-entry bookkeeping. The system described by Pacioli used three books of record—the Memorial, the Journal, and the Ledger. Because of the many forms of money in existence during the medieval period, the Memorial served as the book of original entry in which transactions could be recorded in detail and translated to the money of record (the money used in the Journal and the Ledger) before being recorded in the more official Journal. In describing the Memorial, Pacioli stated that it should include the name of the buyer or seller, the description and price of the goods, the terms of payment, and wherever the receipt or disbursement of cash was involved it should indicate the type of money in which the price was stated and the converted value of that money.[2]

The problems of translating transactions in Pacioli's time continue today—and in greater magnitude, of course—together with the added dilemmas regarding the translation of foreign currency financial statements. Modern times have seen a variety of treatments aimed at dealing with the problem of foreign currency translation. This is due in part to the changing nature of the international operating environment. "Prior to the 1930s the accounting profession made little attempt to establish uniform 'principles' to be followed by those preparing financial statements and reports."[3] However, in response to the stock market crash of 1929, there was an increased emphasis on regulation and investor protection during the 1930s. This led to the development of more uniform guidelines for dealing with the area of foreign currency translation. Unfortunately, these guidelines did not solve a variety of problems related to foreign currency translation. These problems grew out of the needs for translation. Therefore, it is appropriate to examine those needs and the problems they present.

Needs for Translation

In his text, *Accounting Problems of Multinational Enterprises*, Elwood L. Miller discusses six general needs for the translation of foreign currencies. "Each need presents problems that are inherent or that are encountered in producing representative results."[4] The following summary presents the needs and problems as delineated by Miller.

The first need. There is a need to record transactions that are measured or denominated in a foreign currency.
Resulting problems:

1. Which of the several types of exchange rates existing at the time of sale (or purchase) should be used for the transaction?

2. If the exchange rate differs at the time of settlement, how is the difference to be treated?

The second need. There is a need to prepare consolidated statements which report on the economic entity as a whole.
Resulting problems:

1. Which of the multiple exchange rates should be used?

2. How should the resulting imbalances, if any, be treated?

3. Since foreign currency statements are to be translated or denominated in United States dollars, should the underlying transactions also be measured in dollars, that is, as if they had been transacted in the United States?

4. Should the same procedures be required of all United States parent firms regardless of the different circumstances possible (such as operations in countries with unstable currencies)?

5. What is being reflected by the translation process—relative inflation rates, relative purchasing powers of currencies, vagaries of exchange markets, or some mixture of all three?

6. Should the relative price levels within the foreign domiciles be considered?

7. Should price levels and foreign currency translations be considered as separate issues or as parts of one indivisible problem?

The third need. There is a need to evaluate the operations of a foreign business segment.
Resulting problems:

1. Do financial statements lose their relevance when examined outside the context of their particular domiciles?

2. Do translation gains and losses reflect real changes in the economic values of foreign assets?

3. Can or should translation procedures attempt to make foreign operations identical to those conducted in the United States?

4. Can any translation procedure yield relevant data with which to evaluate multiple operating purposes?

5. What information should be furnished external users of financial statements containing translated results of foreign operating segments in order to enable the users to evaluate past operations and their future potentials meaningfully?

The fourth need. There is a need to evaluate the performance of foreign management.
Resulting problems:

1. Does the foreign manager have the opportunity and the authority to protect his segment's investment in United States dollars from erosion by changes in exchange rates?

2. Do changes in exchange rates equate with changes in local asset values and with the local impacts of inflation?

3. Which changes are real and must be managed? Which are illusory or beyond management control?

The fifth need. There is a need to direct and control foreign operations.
Resulting problems:

1. Is there recognition of the fact that translation gains and losses are merely paper gains and losses until conversion takes place and are not real or economic gains and losses?

2. Can a lack of understanding of the true nature of translation gains and losses on the part of management (or investors) lead to actions that result in the incurrence of real or economic losses?

The sixth need. There is a need for translation in order to provide for the convenience of financial statement users.
Resulting problems:

1. Where the financial statements of an independent foreign entity are translated (using a single exchange rate) merely for the convenience of users, should the statements also be adjusted for any differences in the accounting principles existing between the two domiciles?

2. Can convenience translations of foreign-currency statements of independent entities mislead users if the translated statements indicate the domicile whose accounting standards were used to prepare the basic statements?

3. What criteria should be used to assess independence of the entity?

Summary. In response to the various needs for foreign currency translation and the resulting problems, there were a number of official pronouncements issued. These pronouncements will be discussed in the following sections of this chapter.

Related Pronouncements

In December 1931, a special committee on accounting procedures of the American Institute of Accountants issued a report on the treatment of foreign exchange in the accounts of United States corporations. This report was prepared in response to the "numerous and severe fluctuations in foreign exchange,"[5] that occurred during the year. It recommended that:

1. Fixed assets should be converted into dollars at the rates prevailing when such assets were acquired or constructed.

2. Cash, accounts receivable and other miscellaneous current assets should be converted at the rate of exchange prevailing on the date of the balance sheet, unless protected by forward exchange contracts.

3. Current liabilities payable in foreign currency should be converted into dollars at the rate of exchange in force on the date of the balance sheet.

4. Long-term liabilities should be converted at the rate of exchange prevailing when the liability was actually contracted.

5. A loss arising through a fall in foreign exchange was a risk incidental to foreign business, and should be a charge to operating accounts and not a charge to surplus; however, where the item was "substantial" it could be shown separately as a "special" loss. (Gains were not discussed.)

6. Where there were wide fluctuations in exchange, operating statements should be converted at the average rate of exchange applicable to each month or, if this were clerically cumbersome, at a carefully weighted average.

The committee cautioned that the report was only a brief resume of generally accepted principles pertaining to foreign exchange and that, in practice, exceptions would be found. These exceptions were not discussed.

This report later became the basis for *Accounting Research Bulletin No. 4 (ARB No. 4)*, which was issued in 1939. *ARB No. 4* retained the translation process summarized by the earlier report with relatively few modifications. These modifications included:

1. The recommendation that, as in the case of fixed assets, permanent investments and long-term receivables should be translated into dollars at the rates prevailing when such assets were acquired.

2. An exception to the general rule for translating fixed assets, permanent investments and long-term receivables where the asset was acquired shortly before a "substantial" and "presumably permanent" change in the exchange rate with funds obtained in the country concerned — in such a case, it was deemed appropriate to restate the dollar equivalents of such assets to the extent of the change in the related debt.

3. The recommendation that capital stock stated in foreign currency should be translated at the rate of exchange prevailing when it was originally issued.

4. An exception to the general rule for translating long-term debt and capital stock — when long-term debt was incurred or capital stock was issued in connection with the acquisition of fixed assets, permanent investments, or long-term receivables shortly before a "substantial" and "presumably permanent" change in the exchange rate, it was deemed appropriate to state the long-term debt or the capital stock at the new rate and proper to deal with the "exchange difference" as an adjustment to the cost of the acquired asset.

5. The omission in *ARB No. 4* of two hypothetical cases used as examples in the earlier report.

6. The position taken in *ARB No. 4* that foreign "exchange losses" could be appropriately charged to surplus if they resulted from extraordinary developments, such as the devaluations of "worldwide scope and unprecedented magnitude" during the late 1930s, and if their inclusion in the income statement would impair the "significance" of net income and might result in misleading inferences being drawn.

7. The recommendation that, where a major change in an exchange rate took place during the year, more realistic results might be obtained if, in certain situations, income computed in the foreign currency was translated at the new rate for the entire fiscal year. (The situations in which this treatment would be appropriate were not discussed.)

ARB No. 4 also made several additions to the earlier report. These additions included an introductory section, a section on the consolidation of foreign subsidiaries, and a section dealing with gains and losses on foreign exchange.

The introductory section explained that the Bulletin's recommendations applied to United States companies with foreign branches or subsidiaries. It then noted that, due to the uncertain nature of the international operating environment, United States companies should show earnings from foreign operations in their own accounts only to the extent they had been received in the United States. Other recommendations included appropriate provisions for known losses, disclosure of "significant" amounts of unremitted foreign earnings (foreign earnings not yet received in the United States), the establishment of reserves against unremitted foreign earnings to the extent that their "realization" in dollars appeared doubtful, full disclosure in the financial statements of United States companies of the extent to which they included significant foreign items, and the use of care in selecting the most appropriate exchange rate under the circumstances.

The next section questioned the propriety of consolidating foreign subsidiaries. It was noted that, in view of the uncertainty of the values and availability of foreign assets and net income (which were then often subject to controls and exchange restrictions) and the unrealistic income statements that could result from the translation of foreign currencies into dollars, the practice of consolidating foreign statements with United States statements should be seriously questioned. Regardless of whether or not foreign subsidiaries were consolidated with United States operations, it was determined that "adequate disclosure" of foreign operations should be made. The four possible ways suggested for providing this information were:

1. To exclude foreign subsidiaries from consolidation by consolidating domestic statements and furnishing a summary of foreign operations. For foreign subsidiaries, this summary would include their assets and liabilities, their incomes and losses for the year, and the equity of the parent company therein. The total amount of each investment in a foreign subsidiary, along with the basis for its determination, would be shown separately.

2. To consolidate domestic and foreign operations, but supplement the consolidated statements with the summary for foreign operations described above.

3. To furnish two sets of consolidated statements — one which consolidated both foreign and domestic operations and one which consolidated only domestic companies.

4. To consolidate domestic and foreign subsidiaries and furnish separate parent company statements in which the investment in and income from foreign subsidiaries were shown separately from those of domestic subsidiaries.

The section on gains and losses on foreign exchange recommended that realized gains and losses (those differences "realized" upon actual settlement of transactions) should be reflected in current operations. It was also recommended that provisions be made for unrealized gains and losses (those interim "unrealized," or "accounting," differences that are reflected between the time a transaction is recorded and the settlement date, including differences in exchange rates upon the translation of financial statements). While it was suggested that unrealized losses ordinarily be charged against current operations, it was suggested that unrealized gains be carried in a "suspense" account. However, if the unrealized gains offset prior provisions for unrealized losses, it was deemed permissible to credit them to the account previously charged.

In 1953, *ARB No. 4* was restated as Chapter 12, "Foreign Operations and Foreign Exchange," of *ARB No. 43*, "Restatement and Revision of Accounting Research Bulletins." The only change as a result of the restatement was the provision that United States companies should show earnings from foreign operations not only to the extent that the funds were received in the United States but also to the extent that unrestricted funds were available for transmission thereto.

The method of translation promulgated by the 1931 AIA report, *ARB No. 4*, and *ARB No. 43* has been alternatively termed the "AICPA method" and the "current-noncurrent method." The latter name referred to the practice of translating current balance sheet items (current assets and current liabilities) at the current rate (the rate in effect on the balance sheet date) and translating noncurrent balance sheet items (long-term assets, long-term liabilities, and owners' equity) at the "historical" rate (the rate in effect on the transaction date). This method "emphasized conservatism and the subordinate nature of foreign operations following the depression years."[6] Under this method, translation gains and losses resulted from changes in the net-current or working capital position of the foreign operations.

As foreign operations grew from primarily branch operations into full-fledged subsidiaries with on-site manufacturing plants and foreign currency financing, the continued use of the current-noncurrent method was questioned.

By the mid-1950s, inventory accounted for approximately one-fourth of an average foreign operation's total assets.[7] Thus, the method of translating inventory took on an increased level of importance. One of the criticisms of the current-noncurrent method was that by translating inventory at the current rate, it sometimes violated the historical cost concept in United States dollars. It was also noted that the use of the current rate method often violated the lower-of-cost-or-market (LCM) rule in United States dollars where foreign currencies appreciated relative to the dollar. A third criticism was that the use of historical rates to translate long-term debt often only postponed the recognition of gains and losses.[8]

In 1956, one of the critics, Professor Samuel R. Hepworth, proposed the use of the monetary-nonmonetary method of foreign currency translation. Under this method, all monetary assets and liabilities (those fixed in terms of the foreign currency) were to be translated at the current rate, while all nonmonetary assets and liabilities (all others) were to be translated at historical rates. Hepworth reasoned that monetary assets and liabilities involved the receipt or disbursement of a fixed amount of currency and, thus, were subject to fluctuations in the exchange rate; whereas, nonmonetary assets and liabilities were not similarly exposed since any change in money prices could be recovered through adjustments in selling prices. This reasoning assumed the absence of local price controls.[9] Under this method, gains and losses from the translation of net monetary items were to be reflected in current income.

In 1960, a research report published by the National Association of Accountants (NAA) supported Hepworth's position. However, the report modified the original monetary-nonmonetary concept with the recommendation that only realized (conversion) gains (differences which resulted from the actual settlement of transactions) together with all losses be reflected in current income. Unrealized (translation) gains (interim "accounting" differences reflected between the time a transaction was recorded and the date of settlement) were to be deferred, since conservatism directed that potential gains be deferred until realized. This modification complicated the translation process by introducing the problem of determining when exchange gains and losses were realized.[10]

As time passed, actual practice became divided between the approved current-noncurrent method and the not-yet-approved monetary-nonmonetary method. As a result, the Accounting Principles Board (APB) effectively sanctioned the use of the monetary-nonmonetary method as an alternative to the current-noncurrent method in 1965 when it issued *APB Opinion No. 6*, "Status of Accounting Research Bulletins," by accepting the use of the current rate for translation of long-term receivables and long-term liabilities.[11]

During the period following World War II, most foreign currencies experienced a trend of weakening against the United States dollar. Accountants became accustomed to addressing foreign currency translations within an environment replete with conservatism and suspect currencies (the British sterling was devalued by 30 percent in 1949 and there were subsequent devaluations of other European currencies). The general air of conservatism and suspicion was reflected in the practice of giving immediate recognition to translation losses, while deferring translation gains.[12]

With the devaluation of the dollar in 1971, the environment changed, prompting the APB to reconsider the entire dilemma of foreign currency translation. In December of that year, the APB issued an exposure draft proposing the deferral of translation losses to the extent that these losses would apparently be offset by the company's foreign operations in the future. This approach was favorably received, but was never formally endorsed. At the time, the American Institute of Certified Public Accountants was conducting *Accounting Research Study No. 12*, "Reporting Foreign Operations of United States Companies in United States Dollars." The APB decided to wait until the completion of the study before issuing a definitive opinion. During the interim, heavy criticism of the APB resulted in its demise and replacement by the Financial Accounting Standards Board. Two of the main criticisms were that membership on the APB was only a "part-time" position and that members were accountants who had other affiliations and loyalties. Therefore, the independence of the board was questioned. As a result, the APB took no further action on the exposure draft.

At the time the FASB was established in 1973, the United States dollar had been devalued for the second time in two years and the area of foreign currency translation was in disarray. Not only was there a diversity of accounting alternatives in use, but there was a lack of adequate disclosure as well. The crisis nature of the situation was reflected when, in December 1973, the FASB issued as its first official pronouncement, *Financial Accounting Standards Board Statement No. 1*, "Disclosure of Foreign Currency Translation Information." Recognizing the subject was far too complex to deal with on an emergency basis, *Statement No. 1* simply requested that companies maintain consistency in accounting for foreign operations and describe in a footnote the procedures followed and their effects on the financial statements. This statement was not intended to be a final solution to the problem. It was only a stopgap measure, requiring more specific disclosures of foreign currency translation practices and information, thereby providing the FASB time to complete a more thorough review of the area and issue a "final" pronouncement.

FASB *Statement No. 8*

The "final" pronouncement came in the form of *Financial Accounting Standards Board Statement No. 8*, "Accounting for the Translation of Foreign Currency Transactions and Foreign Currency Financial Statements," which was adopted in October 1975. This statement established "standards of financial accounting and reporting for foreign currency transactions in financial statements of a reporting enterprise."[13] It also established "standards of financial accounting and reporting for translating foreign currency financial statements incorporated in the financial statements of an enterprise by consolidation, combination, or the equity method of accounting."[14] Translation of financial statements from one currency to another for some other purpose (such as for the convenience of users) was beyond the scope of the statements.

Standards of Financial Accounting and Reporting

The environment in which this statement was issued was one of continued confusion.

> Multiple methods of translation were in use. Gains and losses were treated in various ways. The adequacy of disclosures was suspect, at best. A consensus did not even exist regarding the appropriate exchange rate to be used where multiple rates existed at a point in time.[15]

As a result, the primary objective of the FASB in issuing *Statement No. 8* was the standardization of foreign currency translation practices and reporting requirements.

Objective of translation. Prior to setting specific standards, the FASB established the following objective:

> The objective of translation is to measure and express (a) in dollars and (b) in conformity with U.S. generally accepted accounting principles the assets, liabilities, revenue, or expenses that are measured or denominated in foreign currency. Remeasuring in dollars the assets, liabilities, revenue, or expenses measured or denominated in foreign currency should not affect either the measurement bases for assets and liabilities or the timing of revenue and expense recognition otherwise required by generally accepted accounting principles.[16]

With this objective in mind, the FASB developed a set of specific standards for the translation of foreign currency transactions and financial statements.

Translation of foreign currency transactions. Before establishing a set of standards for the translation of foreign currency transactions, it was necessary for the FASB to select either the one-transaction or the two-transaction approach. The one-transaction approach viewed the foreign currency transaction as incomplete until settlement was made. Under this approach, the "exchange" risk was included as part of the transaction risk. Therefore, any differences resulting from a change in exchange rates between the transaction date and the settlement date (conversion gains and losses) were accounted for by adjusting the original selling (or purchase) prices of the items sold (or acquired).

The two-transaction approach, on the other hand, viewed the foreign currency transaction as two separate events—the sale (or purchase) and the subsequent settlement. Under this approach, the "exchange" risk was considered separately from the sale (or purchase). Therefore, any difference resulting from a change in exchange rates between the transaction date and the settlement date was considered the result of a separate interim event—a change in the exchange rate—and accounted for as a conversion gain or loss.

The FASB selected the two-transaction approach. Specifically, in rejecting the one-transaction view, the Board rejected the idea that the reported revenue from an export sale or the cost of an imported asset was affected by later changes in the related receivable or payable. They reasoned that the "exchange" exposure involved in a foreign currency transaction stemmed from the delay in payment, not the sale or purchase. If immediate settlement were made, no "exchange" gain or loss would occur. Therefore, management's decision to defer settlement creates the exposure to subsequent gains or losses and the results of that decision should be reflected separately.

Once the FASB selected the two-transaction approach, their next step was to establish standards for the translation of foreign currency transactions. In so doing, the transactions were grouped into three categories: (1) closed transactions, (2) open transactions at balance sheet date, and (3) settlement of transactions open on the preceding balance sheet date [those items in (2)] in the next fiscal year.

Closed transactions— —Where a transaction was initiated and settled in the same period, it was a closed transaction. If the exchange rate changed between the transaction date and the settlement date, the resulting difference was to be accounted for as a conversion gain or loss and included in current income.

Open transactions— —If there was a balance sheet date between the transaction date and the settlement date, the transaction was considered to be open. These transactions were also considered to be exposed to changes in rates at the balance sheet date. Since these changes were regarded as separate, significant events, the resulting adjustments were to be treated as exchange gains or losses and recognized in the current period.

Transactions settled after intervening balance sheet date— —In addition, if the exchange rate changed between the balance sheet date and the settlement date, the dollar amount of the item also differed and a conversion gain or loss resulted. This difference was to be recognized as a gain or loss in the current period and not netted against or combined with the first transaction.

Translation of foreign currency financial statements. The assets, liabilities, revenues and expenses in foreign financial statements were initially measured and recorded in foreign currencies and might not have been accounted for in accordance with United States generally accepted accounting principles (GAAP). Therefore, the first step in the translation process required by FASB *Statement No. 8* called for restatement (any adjustments necessary to bring the foreign financial statements into conformity with United States GAAP). The second step specified how those financial statements were to be translated into dollars.

In effect, the first step reconstructed the statements *as if* the supporting transactions had been made in the United States.

For the second step (translation), the FASB specified the use of the temporal method, since it was considered to be amenable to any method of reporting, whether cost- or value-based. Amounts carried at past prices (their historical costs) on foreign financial statements were to be translated using the exchange rates in effect at their acquisition dates. The amounts carried at present or future prices (current market prices or net realizable values) on the foreign statements were to be translated using the current rate (that in effect on the balance sheet date). Accounts representing cash, receivables, or payables carried on the foreign financial statements that were denominated in something other than the local currency were to be restated in terms of the local currency using the appropriate current exchange rate (the exchange rate between the two currencies in effect on the balance sheet date). These restated accounts were then to be translated into dollars using the current exchange rate between the local currency and dollars.

Theoretically, all revenue and expense transactions were to be translated using the exchange rate in effect on the date each transaction occurred. Since it usually was impractical to translate each transaction separately, revenue and expenses were to be translated using a weighted average exchange rate covering the reporting period. However, revenue and expenses that related to specific assets and liabilities translated at historic rates were also to be translated at those historic rates — depreciation and amortization were common examples.

Recognition of translation gains and losses. Any differences in the translated dollar balances of the asset and liability accounts since the last balance sheet date (or since the date of acquisition where no intervening balance sheet date occurred) which were due to changes in the exchange rates used for translation were to be recognized as translation gains or losses and included in current income. Such gains and losses were not to be deferred to a later period.

Separate disclosure of translation gains and losses was not recommended. Instead, such gains and losses were to be reported in the financial statements or a footnote as part of the aggregate "exchange" gain or loss included in determining net income for the period.

Application to interim financial statements. Statement No. 8 applied to interim as well as year-end financial statements. As such, any translation gains or losses which occurred during the interim period could not be deferred. This was in accordance with *APB Opinion No. 28*, "Interim Financial Reporting," which stated: "Gains and losses that arise in any interim period similar to those that would not be deferred at year-end should not be deferred to later interim periods within the same fiscal year."

Applying the lower-of-cost-or-market rule. In applying the lower-of-cost-or-market rule (LCM), *Statement No. 8* required that the test be applied to translated dollar amounts. That is, the historical cost of an inventory in translated dollars must be compared to the current market price of the inventory in translated dollars. This departure from the normal translation process outlined by *Statement No. 8* sometimes produced results that differed from those that would have been produced under the normal translation process. For example, assume that United States parent company (A) had a foreign subsidiary (B). Further assume that B had inventory with a historical cost of FCU 8,000 (i.e., 8,000 foreign currency units) and a market price of FCU 10,000. At the time the inventory was acquired, the exchange rate was $1 U.S. = FCU 1 (historic rate). At the time of translation, the exchange rate was $.70 U.S. = FCU 1 (current rate). If the LCM rule was applied to the inventory as stated in FCU and then translated (according to the normal translation process), the translated inventory amount would have been the translated historical cost $8,000 (FCU 8,000 × $1 ÷ FCU 1 = $8,000). However, if the LCM rule was applied to the translated cost and market price of B's inventory (according to the specified approach) the translated dollar amount of inventory would have been $7,000 (FCU 10,000 × $.70 ÷ FCU 1 = $7,000). This procedure was intended to produce dollar measurements which were in conformity with United States generally accepted accounting principles (i.e., the LCM rule would be applied in United States dollars), whereas the normal translation process would not do so in certain circumstances.

Other matters which will not be considered. Statement No. 8 also provided guidelines for the income tax consequences of rate changes and forward exchange contracts (amended in December 1977 by FASB *Statement No. 20*, "Accounting for Forward Exchange Contracts"). However, these are considered to be specialized requirements and will not be considered in this book.

Disclosures required. Interim or year-end financial statements were to disclose the aggregate translation or conversion gain or loss included in determining the net income for the periods. Also, if it were practical to do so, any other effects of changes in exchange rates on the reported results of operations were to be described and quantified. Examples of other effects included the aggregate amount of tax effects related to exchange gains or losses and the effects of rate changes on reported revenue and earnings (including effects on selling prices, sales volume, and cost structures). Finally, where the exchange rates changed after the end of the reporting period, the financial statements were not required to be adjusted to reflect the changes. However, if the effect was considered to be significant, it might be necessary to disclose the amount of the rate change and its effects on the financial statements in the footnotes.

Translation for convenience. Translations of the financial statements of foreign companies for purposes other than for use in consolidation, combination, or the equity method of accounting were specifically exempted from the requirements of *Statement No. 8*. A prime example given was the translation of foreign financial statements for the convenience of statement users where the translated statements were to stand alone.

Summary

In summary, *Statement No. 8* standardized foreign currency translation by requiring the use of the temporal method of translation. Unfortunately, in doing so, the FASB opted for standardization at the expense of realism. The general discontent (if not anger) with the Statement pressured the FASB to reconsider. When the FASB called for comments on *Statement Nos. 1–12*, most of the responses expressed dissatisfaction with *Statement No. 8*. The review process which followed called into question the theoretical validity of *Statement No. 8*, along with the soundness of its objectives.[17] Subsequently, the FASB abandoned the dollar perspective used in *Statement No. 8*, and with it the decision *not* to produce an exchange gain or loss which was compatible with the expected economic effect of a change in the exchange rate.

FASB Statement No. 52

Adopted in December 1981, *Financial Accounting Standards Board Statement No. 52*, "Foreign Currency Translation," established

> revise[d] standards of financial accounting and reporting for foreign currency transactions in financial statements of a reporting enterprise. . . . It also revised the standards for translating foreign currency financial statements . . . that [were] incorporated in the financial statements of an enterprise by consolidation, combination, or the equity method of accounting.[18]

Translations of financial statements from one currency to another for some other purpose were beyond the scope of the Statement.

Statement No. 52 superseded the following pronouncements: FASB *Statement No. 8*, "Accounting for the Translation of Foreign Currency Transactions and Foreign Currency Financial Statements"; FASB *Statement No. 20*, "Accounting for Forward Exchange Contracts"; FASB *Interpretation No. 15*, "Translation of Unamortized Policy Acquisition Costs by a Stock Life Insurance Company"; and FASB *Interpretation No. 17*, "Applying the Lower of Cost or Market Rule in Translated Financial Statements."

Standards of Financial Accounting and Reporting

The changes in the standards of accounting and reporting promulgated in *Statement No. 52* from those promulgated in *Statement No. 8* emanated from a change in the objectives of translation. By adopting a "functional currency" perspective, the FASB laid the groundwork for the application of two alternative methods of translation. When the foreign currency was the functional currency, the current rate method of translation would be used. When the reporting currency (the dollar) was the functional currency, the temporal (*Statement No. 8*) method of translation would be used.

Objectives of translation. According to *Statement No. 52*, the translation of foreign financial statements should accomplish the following objectives:

a. Provide information that is generally compatible with the expected economic effects of a rate change on an enterprise's cash flows and equity.

b. Reflect in consolidated statements the financial results and relationships of the individual consolidated entities as measured in their functional currencies in conformity with U.S. generally accepted accounting principles.[19]

The functional currency. Statement No. 52 adopted the functional currency approach to translating foreign financial statements. Using this approach, the first step in the translation process required determination of the functional currency of each entity to be included in the financial statements of an enterprise by consolidation, combination, or the equity method. The functional currency of an entity was defined as "the currency of the primary economic environment in which the entity operates; normally, that is the currency of the environment in which an entity primarily generates and expends cash."[20] Several clear-cut examples were given.

If an entity's operations were self-contained and integrated within a particular country, the functional currency of that entity would generally be the currency of the country in which the entity was located. However, if the foreign entity was an integral part of the parent company's operations, the functional currency of the foreign entity would probably be that of the parent company. (An example of such an "integral part" would be a foreign division, branch, or subsidiary that primarily manufactures a subassembly that is shipped to a United States plant for inclusion in a product to be sold to customers in the United States or in other parts of the world.) Also, if a foreign entity had separate and distinct operations existing in different economic environments, each of these operations might well have a different functional currency. Finally, if the operating environment of the foreign entity was classified as "highly inflationary" by *Statement No. 52*, the functional currency of that entity would be assumed to be the same as the reporting currency of the parent.

When a foreign functional currency has experienced a three-year cumulative inflation rate of "approximately 100 percent or more"[21] (an annual rate of 26 percent would produce a three-year cumulative rate of 100 percent), the financial statements of the foreign entity should be remeasured as if the reporting currency were the functional currency. Table 1 presents a summary of major United States trading partners (countries) and their three-year cumulative inflation rates at the time *Statement No. 52* was published (December 1981).

Generally, an entity's functional currency would be based on observable facts. However, where the facts did not clearly indicate the functional currency, management's judgment as to which currency would measure the financial results and relationships of the foreign entity with the greatest degree of relevance and reliability would have to be used in determining the functional currency.

Once the determination of the functional currency was made, it was to be used consistently unless significant changes in the economic facts and circumstances involving the entity clearly indicated the need for a change in

Table 1. Three-Year Cumulative Inflation Rates of
Major United States Trading Partners

Country	Three Year Cumulative Inflation Rate 1981
Brazil*	573.6%
Mexico**	91.1
Italy	63.8
Venezuela	58.8
United Kingdom	49.7
Republic of South Africa	48.3
Egypt	46.6
France	42.2
Canada	35.1
Australia	31.8
Japan	17.4
Germany	16.3

*By definition, a "highly inflationary economy."
**On the brink of a "highly inflationary economy."
(Source: International Financial Statistics XXXV (December 1982): 51).

the functional currency. Should a change in the functional currency be made, previously issued financial statements were not to be restated.

FASB *Statement No. 52* required that the assets, liabilities, and results of operations of an entity be measured using the entity's functional currency. Therefore, if an entity's accounts were not maintained in its functional currency, remeasurement was required before translation into the reporting currency.[22] This remeasurement process was meant "to produce the same result as if the entity's books of record had been maintained in the functional currency."[23] The process used to accomplish this was essentially the FASB *Statement No. 8* method of translation. Thus, where the functional currency is also the reporting currency, the need for remeasurement was eliminated.

Translation of foreign currency financial statements. Two methods of translation were specified by *Statement No. 52* — dependent upon the functional currency — with two dissimilar treatments of the resulting differences ("exchange gains and losses").

Foreign currency is functional — — Where a foreign entity's functional currency is the local currency or some other foreign currency, the foreign financial statements were to be translated into United States dollars using the current rate method. Under this method, as stated earlier, all assets and liabilities are translated at the exchange rate in effect on the balance sheet date. Revenues, expenses, gains, and losses should be translated using the exchange rate in effect on the date the item was recognized. However, since this is usually impractical due to the large number of items involved, income statement items are generally translated using an appropriately weighted average exchange rate for the period.

The resulting translation adjustments are not to be included in the determination of net income, but are to be deferred and are to be reported separately and accumulated in a separate component of stockholders equity. The FASB suggested this component could be titled "Equity Adjustment from Foreign Currency Translation" or something similar. Upon the sale or the complete (or substantially complete) liquidation of an investment in a foreign entity, the portion of the translation adjustment attributable to that entity should be removed from stockholders equity and included in the determination of the gain or loss on the sale or liquidation of the investment for the period in which the sale or liquidation occurs.

United States dollar is functional currency — — Where a foreign entity's functional currency is the United States dollar, the foreign financial statements are to be remeasured in United States dollars using essentially the same method as was required for translation by *Statement No. 8*. Since this remeasurement process will have converted the foreign financial statements from the foreign currency (in which the records are kept) to the United States dollar (which serves as both the functional and reporting currency), there is no need for additional translation from the functional currency to the reporting currency using the current rate method. (Exceptions to the

Statement No. 8 method of translation are that, under *Statement No. 52*, a foreign entity's deferred income taxes and the unamortized policy acquisition costs of a stock life insurance company must be translated at the current rate.)

The translation adjustments resulting from the remeasurement process used where the functional currency of the foreign entity is the United States dollar are to be made directly to income in the year of the adjustment. Therefore, the results achieved using this remeasurement process are essentially the same as those that would have been achieved under FASB *Statement No. 8.*

Foreign currency transactions. Statement No. 52 defined foreign currency transactions as those "denominated in a currency other than the entity's functional currency."[24]

For all foreign currency transactions (other than foreign exchange contracts), this Statement required that, on the date the transaction is recognized, each asset, liability, revenue, expense, gain, or loss arising from the transaction is to be measured and recorded in the functional currency of the recording entity. This is to be done using the exchange rate in effect on that date at which the transaction could have been settled. At each balance sheet date, recorded balances of financial statement elements that are denominated in a currency other than the functional currency of the recording entity are to be adjusted to reflect the exchange rate at which that element could be settled as of that date (usually the exchange rate in effect on the balance sheet date). On the settlement date of a foreign currency transaction the amount of the settlement should be measured and recorded in the functional currency of the recording entity. This will be done using the actual exchange rate at which the transaction was settled.

When foreign currency transactions result in receivables or payables that are fixed in terms of a foreign currency, a change in the exchange rate between the functional currency and the foreign currency in which the transaction is denominated will result in an increase or decrease in the amount of the functional currency required to settle the transaction. An increase in this amount will result in a "transaction loss," whereas a decrease in this amount will result in a "transaction gain." When the exchange rate changes between the transaction date and the balance sheet date, the resulting "transaction gain or loss" will generally be included in the determination of net income for the period in which the exchange rate changes. Likewise, when the exchange rate changes between the transaction date (or an intervening balance sheet date) and the settlement date, the "transaction gain or loss" that is realized upon settlement of the foreign currency transaction will generally be included in the determination of net income for the period in which the transaction is settled.

Not all "transaction gains and losses" were to be included in the determination of net income. Two specific exceptions noted in *Statement No. 52* were: (1) foreign currency transactions that are designated and effective as economic hedges of a net investment in a foreign entity, and (2) intercompany foreign currency transactions that are of a long-term investment nature if the entities involved in the transaction are consolidated, combined, or accounted for by the equity method on the reporting enterprise's financial statements. In both instances, gains and losses resulting from these types of foreign currency transactions should be reported in the same manner as translation adjustments: that is, reported separately and accumulated in a separate component of equity rather than being included in the determination of net income.

Other matters. In the case of sales or transfers between entities which are consolidated, combined, or accounted for by the equity method on the financial statements of the enterprise, the elimination of the resulting intercompany profits should be based on the exchange rates in effect on the dates of the sales or transfers. If this is impractical, an appropriate weighted average or approximation may be used.

In general, the exchange rates in effect on the balance sheet date and on the various transaction dates are used in the translation process. If for some reason the exchangeability between two currencies is lacking on one of these dates, the exchange rate in effect on the date exchangeability is restored should be used. If exchangeability between the two currencies is other than temporary, the propriety of consolidating, combining, or using the equity method of accounting for the foreign entity should be questioned.

Normally there is more than one exchange rate between two currencies on any given date. In translating foreign currency transactions, the rate at which the transaction could have been settled should be used. In translating foreign financial statements, the exchange applicable to conversions of currency for dividend remittances should be used.

Where detailed record keeping and computations would become burdensome, the use of averages and approximations are acceptable as long as the results produced are reasonable approximations.

As stated earlier, *Statement No. 52* also supersedes FASB *Statement No. 8* and FASB *Statement No. 20* in the area of accounting for forward exchange contracts and the income tax consequences of exchange rate changes. Due to the fact that these are specialized areas which are not considered in detail in this book, the related requirements will not be summarized. However, it can be said that a forward exchange contract is an agreement to exchange different currencies at a specified rate on a specified future date. As such, forward exchange contracts are a special type of foreign currency transaction. When a forward exchange contract is designated and effective as a hedge against a net foreign investment or a firm foreign currency commitment, the translation adjustment (gain or loss) is generally made to stockholders' equity (in the case of an investment) or to the basis of the transaction being hedged (in the case of a commitment). A gain or loss on a forward exchange contract that does not qualify as an economic hedge should be included in the determination of net income in accordance with the requirements for other foreign currency transactions. The rules of interperiod income tax allocation generally apply in this area.

Disclosure. The aggregate transaction gain or loss included in the determination of net income for the period should be disclosed in the financial statements or the accompanying footnotes. No further specific guidance was given.

An analysis of the changes in the translation component of stockholders' equity should be provided in a separate financial statement, in a footnote to the financial statements, or in the statement of changes in equity. At a minimum this analysis must include:

1. The beginning and ending amount of cumulative translation adjustment;

2. The aggregate adjustment for the period resulting from the translation of foreign currency financial statements and the gains or losses from certain hedging and intercompany transactions;

3. The amount of income taxes for the period allocated to the translation adjustments reported in a separate component of stockholders' equity;

4. The amounts transferred from the cumulative translation adjustments in stockholders' equity and included in the determination of net income for the period as a result of the sale or substantial or complete liquidation of an investment in a foreign entity.

While an enterprise's financial statements should not be adjusted for a change in the exchange rate occurring after balance sheet date, the rate change and its effects on unsettled foreign currency transactions balances should be disclosed if they are significant.

Conclusion

Having reviewed the pertinent FASB statements, the next step in this examination of the area of foreign currency translation will be to review the related accounting literature. Not only will such a review be helpful in highlighting the strengths and weaknesses of *Statement No. 8* and *Statement No. 52*, but it should also provide insights into ways in which accounting for foreign currency translation could be improved.

4

Literature Review and Critical Analysis

Introduction

In addition to being the subject of the official pronouncements already discussed, foreign currency translation has received extensive treatment in the literature, particularly following the developments of the early 1970s which saw the devaluation of the dollar and the movement to a system of floating exchange rates. A review of this literature reveals that the pertinent articles can be divided into the following nine main topical areas which are to be covered in this chapter:

1. The provisions of FASB *Statement No. 8*;

2. The accounting issues in *Statement No. 8*;

3. The tax aspects of *Statement No. 8*;

4. The effect of *Statement No. 8* on the financial results of specific multinational corporations;

5. The effects of *Statement No. 8* on multinational corporations in general;

6. The impact of *Statement No. 8* on financial statement analysis;

7. Managing and controlling the accounting and/or economic risk of exchange rate changes;

8. FASB *Statement No. 52* and related topics;

9. The conceptual issues underlying foreign currency accounting and reporting.

The Provisions of FASB *Statement No. 8*

Since 1975, a plethora of articles describing the technical provisions of *Statement No. 8* has been published. Some of these articles, such as those by

Philip E. Meyer,[1] and by Raymond J. Clay and William W. Holder,[2] have been purely descriptive. They served to enlighten the financial statement user regarding the requirements set forth by the statement.

Other articles, such as that by John Gray,[3] were not only descriptive but also offered an introduction to some of the issues concerning foreign currency translation which were expanded upon in later works. Those areas touched on by Gray included the possible reversal of balance sheet exposure, erratic swings in earnings, and the increased activity in the international hedging and financing areas. Gray noted that those opposed to the statement criticized it for resulting in a "misleading and erratic interpretation of profit performance."[4] Analysts complained that "the job of determining the quality of reported earnings and forecasting future earnings of multinational companies (was) much more difficult and, in some cases, nearly impossible."[5] However, proponents of the statement took a different view. They claimed that the statement had made it easier to evaluate the performance of multinational corporations, since alternative practices had been eliminated and all companies were reporting on the same basis. Further, proponents contended that the erratic swings in earnings merely reflected the risks inherent in international operations under a system of floating exchange rates.

Initially, both arguments appear to have merit. Nevertheless, upon closer examination the proponents' arguments break down. What many proponents failed to consider was the fact that the term "exchange gains and losses" was made a nebulous hodge-podge by *Statement No. 8*. It was much like a wastebasket that contained conversion (realized) gains and losses as well as translation (unrealized) differences. The latter could often be further subdivided into differences that: (1) might be realized in the near future (on current items), (2) might be realized some time downstream (on less current items), (3) might never occur (on long-term items). Furthermore, most multinational companies dealt in various bundles of foreign currencies having different volatilities in both frequency and magnitude. To argue that any single amount labeled as "exchange gains and losses" purports to represent the past and future "risks inherent in international operations" requires a vivid imagination indeed.

Regarding the uniformity argument, the mere fact that all statement issuers must follow unsound practices hardly makes them correct.

The Accounting Issues in FASB *Statement No. 8*

In 1977, Clyde P. Stickney and Harold E. Wyman examined some of the accounting issues in FASB *Statement No. 8*. They noted that as a result of the statement some economically poor decisions were being reported as good decisions in the external financial statements. Their major criticism was that the translation methodology prescribed by the statement implicitly assumed that "monetary items are exposed to exchange gains and losses while nonmonetary items are not exposed."[6] Stickney and Wyman found four main weaknesses in *Statement No. 8*'s translation methodology resulting from this underlying assumption about exposure.

First of all, Stickney and Wyman noted that "an exchange gain or loss is recognized on every transaction affecting a monetary asset or liability regardless of whether an actual conversion of foreign currency was required during the current period or will be required in a future period."[7] Thus, *Statement No. 8* makes the assumption that "items giving rise to translation, as opposed to transaction, gains and losses are always exposed."[8]

Secondly, the translation methodology employed by the statement

> fails to recognize potential exchange gains and losses when a foreign unit borrows or lends and denominates the obligation in United States dollars. . . . There is a very real exposure to the foreign unit, however, if its currency appreciates or depreciates relative to the dollar while the obligation is outstanding.[9]

Thirdly, the statement's methodology for measuring exchange exposure assumes that "a monetary item requiring a currency conversion is exposed just because an exchange gain or loss is recognized on it. Consideration must be given to the possibility that the monetary item has already been implicitly hedged in setting the interest rate on the obligation."[10]

Fourthly, nonmonetary items are "presumed not to be exposed since an exchange gain or loss is not calculated on them."[11] However, as Stickney and Wyman pointed out, this was not always true. For example, inventory which is a nonmonetary item may, in some cases, be the most exposed asset in the firm.

The authors concluded that the methodology used by FASB *Statement No. 8* to measure exchange exposure was not particularly useful. Instead, they suggested that "the appropriate dimensions for measuring the exposure of an asset or liability appear to be (1) whether an actual currency conversion is required to settle an obligation, and (2) whether the item is to be held for several years or for a much shorter period of time."[12] However, in light of the reporting requirements of the statement, management may feel compelled to make ill-advised economic decisions in an attempt to hedge against translation losses and protect the "bottom line" in the income statement. Therefore, Stickney and Wyman proposed that the reporting of "exchange gains and losses" be improved through the use of footnote disclosure. In their view, the exchange gain or loss should be divided into its various elements so that investors could identify the real and nominal components.

In his January 1978 article, Marvin M. Deupree noted that another weakness of FASB *Statement No. 8* was that, due to the "yo-yo" effect upon earnings, "the reader of the financial statements has no firm basis on which to judge the trend of the company's results of operations."[13] According to Deupree, problems such as this could have been avoided if the FASB had performed a more thorough analysis of the underlying accounting principles upon which the statement is based. In his estimation, "there were two particularly critical principles not adequately pursued in *FASB #8*: (1) the definition of losses/gains and its application to translation of monetary items, and (2) the definition of cost and its application."[14]

Deupree reasoned that the public expected any gain or loss reported in net income to be associated with a discernible, corresponding change in the company's economic worth. Therefore, by requiring unrealized translation gains and losses (which had no real economic substance) to be reported in income, the FASB set the stage for additional criticisms. On the other hand, if the Board had prepared a detailed technical analysis of the nature of the changes resulting from foreign currency translation, they could have used the results along with their definition of gains and losses to defend the accounting policies which were developed in that area.

In the area of cost, Deupree suggested that the FASB would have done better to adopt a "sacrifices" concept of cost (defining cost as the "sacrifice" made for an asset or service) rather than selecting and applying a definition which bound cost to the supplier's invoice amount. Deupree claimed that the reason the FASB rejected the "sacrifices" concept of cost was that they feared that the approach would lead to the deferral of gains and losses. Instead, he contended, it would have merely distinguished between costs and losses (or gains) and, thus, made it possible for a company to account for items based on their classification.

It was Deupree's conclusion that, as a result of the FASB's failure to re-examine certain basic accounting principles involved in foreign currency translation, "the explanations in *FASB #8* based on accounting principles are in key instances shallow and not persuasively supportive of the accounting conclusions."[15]

One year later, in January of 1979, *Business Week* presented an article dealing with the FASB's review of *Statement No. 8*. This review was undertaken as part of a general review of the Board's first twelve pronouncements. However, it was *Statement No. 8* that drew the most criticism. One of the major criticisms was that the statement looked at foreign operations "as if they might be liquidated tomorrow rather than as an ongoing business."[16] It was noted that an "exchange" gain in one quarter was often erased by a loss in the next quarter and that "sizable chunks" of these "paper" entries might never be realized.

Other criticisms dealt with the mismatching of costs and revenues resulting from translations of inventory and foreign debt. Inventories were translated at the appropriate historic exchange rates while sales were translated at their average current exchange rates. This resulted in profit margins being misstated and gave both investors and managements misleading signals. Another problem concerned the large translation swings associated with foreign debt. "As with inventories, the problem was compounded by the fact that while long-term debt was translated at current exchange rates, the plant and equipment often associated with that debt had to be translated at historical rates."[17] Moreover, critics charged that frequently, under *Statement No. 8*, a translation loss indicated an economic gain and a translation gain indicated an economic loss. This criticism alludes to the unreal differences that can develop between earnings as reported by the foreign operation and earnings as reported in translated dollars. These differences developed as a result of the temporal method of translation — which required that inventories (carried at cost) and fixed assets of foreign operations be translated using historic rates, while the debt used to finance these items was required to be translated at the current rate.

The example used by *Business Week* to illustrate the above criticism involved a United States corporation with foreign operations in Germany. It was explained that if the German mark strengthened against the United States dollar many individuals would reason that an "economic gain" had occurred because the foreign assets would usually be worth more in United States dollars and the foreign sales and profits could also be worth more in United States dollars. However, it was also explained that under *Statement No. 8*, the company could show an "accounting loss" (translation loss) due to an increase in net liabilities as stated in United States dollars. Here the underlying rationale was that it would take more in United States dollars to pay off the debt. What *Business Week* did not mention was the fact that in most cases the foreign debt was repaid using foreign currencies and not United States dollars.

Business Week also suggested that the FASB could reduce the "earnings sting" of foreign currency gyrations by rearranging the income statement. "Translation gains or losses could be separated from a company's operating income and shown on a separate line."[18]

Later in 1979, Gerald I. White also discussed the volatility of earnings resulting from *Statement No. 8*'s requirement that all translation gains and losses be recognized as part of earnings on a quarterly basis.[19] He concluded that permitting any leeway in the recognition of translation "gains and losses" on the grounds that they were only temporary would be unacceptable due to possible abuse. Instead, he suggested that these gains and losses could be recognized only on an annual basis (eliminating those effects that reverse during the year) or that they could be debited or credited directly to stockholders' equity. However, White also recognized that his alternatives are not without their own problems. The first alternative would do nothing to alleviate earnings volatility on an annual basis. The second alternative would violate the "clean surplus" concept of income that has been an important tenet of GAAP.

Two other topics discussed by White were those of hedging and disclosure. In discussing hedging, White noted "a firm that is economically hedged can nonetheless show unrealized accounting gains or losses. On the other hand, measures taken to hedge accounting risks may create unrecognized economic risks or impose unnecessary costs on the firm."[20] The previous example of a United States corporation financing foreign assets with foreign debt denominated in the same foreign currency can also be used here. By financing its German assets with debt denominated in marks, a United States corporation could be considered economically hedged. If the mark strengthened against the dollar, the foreign operations could still pay off the foreign debt with profits earned in marks. Thus, the firm could be considered to be economically hedged. However, since the foreign assets would be translated using historic rates and the foreign debt would be translated using current rates, the firm could show unrealized accounting losses. In order to hedge its accounting risks, the firm could resort to forward-exchange contracts which would involve both an economic cost and future economic risk (if the foreign exchange rates moved in the opposite direction of that anticipated).

White also noted that the disclosure requirements of the statement were very weak and should be improved. White pointed out that, while *Statement No. 8* required companies to disclose the aggregate exchange gain or loss included in income, the statement did not specify where the disclosures were to be presented. Additionally, the statement did not specify whether the disclosed item should be before or after taxes. Since relatively few corporate reports volunteered that information, analyzing the effect of the "exchange gain or loss" on the financial reports was more difficult and comparability was impaired.

More important, in White's estimation, was the fact that only a few companies disclosed the income statement effects of translation. He attributed this lack of disclosure to a flaw in *Statement No. 8*'s requirement that companies disclose such effects "if practical." By including the qualifier, "if practical," the FASB provided a convenient excuse for companies to omit this type of disclosure. White admitted it was difficult to quantify the effects of changing exchange rates on revenue, cost of goods sold, and other line items in the income statement. However, he concluded that the effects of translation on the income statement were too important not to be shown.

The Tax Aspects of FASB *Statement No. 8*

In 1976, Marvin N. Schmitz examined the area of taxation as related to foreign "exchange gains and losses." At that time, he observed that a foreign "exchange gain or loss" could be recognized for tax purposes only if a sale, exchange conversion, or other closed transaction had taken place.[21]

Tax aspects were subsequently addressed in greater detail by Michael L. Moore and John L. Kramer. In their 1977 article, they examined the United States tax rules regarding the translation of foreign currency transactions and the reporting of foreign activities. They also reviewed the requirements of FASB *Statement No. 8* and noted that the tax and accounting treatments of this area differed.[22]

"Tax laws specify five methods of translation: the specific transactions method, the profit and loss method, the net worth method, the foreign corporation method, and the Subpart F (or controlled foreign corporation method), each applying to a specific situation."[23] The authors pointed out that the appropriate tax method of translation would depend on the circumstances, such as the entity used to conduct the foreign activities, the frequency of the activities, and the type of transaction. Moore and Kramer then discussed each of the translation methods used for tax purposes in detail, gave examples of each, and indicated where and how they differed from the translation methods prescribed by *Statement No. 8*. Typically, tax and accounting differences resulted from dissimilar realization assumptions.

The differences in the tax and accounting treatments of foreign "exchange gains and losses" led to the need for interperiod income tax allocation. These differences were often included in deferred income taxes in consolidated balance sheets. Once recorded, unless the foreign "exchange gains and losses" were eventually realized or subsequently adjusted, the resulting deferred income taxes could become permanent items.

The fact that the translation method used for tax purposes and the tax deductibility of "exchange gains and losses" depended on the circumstances might have led multinational corporations to structure their foreign activities in a way that would allow them to receive the favored tax treatment. This in itself was not negative, since taxation was an important factor. However, if tax planning considerations took precedence over sound business practices, the corporation as a whole could suffer as a result.

The Effect of FASB *Statement No. 8* on the Financial Results of Specific Multinational Corporations

In 1976, *Forbes* presented an article criticizing *Statement No. 8* for distorting reality.[24] It was noted that the inclusion of translation gains and losses in quarterly earnings during periods of wildly gyrating exchange rates could make quarterly reports look like "a profile of the Swiss Alps,"[25] even if the applicable exchange rate ended the year where it began. Company executives claimed that "this sort of thing baffles investors and even sophisticated analysts . . . by obscuring the real trend of a company."[26] It was also noted that, depending on the makeup of the balance sheet, companies were producing widely different sets of quarterly earnings even in the same industry. For example, "Honeywell reported a 1,200% gain for the first quarter of 1976; Sperry Rand, with a slightly larger revenue rise, showed only 11% higher net."[27]

Despite these aberrations, the FASB continued to claim that it was not the function of accounting to smooth reported earnings, since they were based upon historical events. Instead, they said that it would be artificial to defer any of these translation gains and losses. What the FASB apparently refused to consider was that a large portion of these gains and losses were not real. As such, their premature recognition tended to cloud rather than clarify matters. A similar assessment was made by Richard R. Stover, health care analyst for Mitchell, Hutchins, who stated that

> *FASB 8* only made it more difficult to gauge and measure quarterly operating trends of companies. The historical treatment of inventories distorts gross margin trends. An analyst wants to see if they are deteriorating or improving quarter by quarter. So you have to depend on the company and how much more it is willing to disclose, which can vary.[28]

The controversy surrounding *Statement No. 8* was not merely viewed as an esoteric argument between the opponents and proponents of the statement regarding what was or was not real. *Statement No. 8* could affect the way multinationals did business. For example, Marshall A. Petersen, treasurer of TRW Inc., cited that "many companies have been borrowing or hedging in local currencies to keep the fluctuations off the earnings report. Some companies tried to tie prices to currency."[29]

The effectiveness of such measures would depend on the circumstances. Some operating environments are simply not suited to such solutions. In addition, hedging and borrowing carry economic costs.

In 1978, *Forbes* presented further evidence of what was termed the "foolishness" and "perniciousness" of *Statement No. 8*.[30] It was noted that in the case of Royal Dutch/Shell Group, "*FASB 8* forced the company to reduce its first three-month earnings by a staggering $510 million. Reported year-to-year earnings slumped 98%. In fact, real operating earnings dropped by 39%."[31] Situations such as this, which were not at all uncommon, resulted in M.S. Forbes, Jr. commenting that "countless millions of dollars are being spent in borrowing and hedging to minimize earnings volatility. Even investment decisions are being affected by this rule. *FASB 8* is so utterly lacking in common sense that it should be scrapped immediately."[32]

The Effects of FASB *Statement No. 8* on Multinational Corporations in General

In an earlier review of the Statement's possible undesirable effects, William D. Serfass noted that including the translation gains and losses in current income, as required by the statement, resulted in earnings fluctuations which did not properly measure the economic results of a business.[33] He also noted that, during a volatile floating foreign exchange market, the translation of foreign financial statements in accordance with *Statement No. 8* resulted in "distortions of the operational results, thereby contradicting the statement's primary objective that such remeasurement should not affect the measurement bases for assets and liabilities or the timing of revenue and expense recognition."[34] Serfass held that the translation process actually resulted in the revaluation of foreign assets and liabilities.

Another criticism leveled by Serfass was that "the required recognition of translation adjustments in operations also could seriously hamper good business judgment by obligating management to engage in costly foreign exchange protection programs to protect itself from adverse 'bookkeeping' adjustments."[35] To support this statement, he gave the example that, in 1974, International Telephone and Telegraph attempted to cover its balance sheet exposure by selling $600 million worth of foreign currencies in the foreign exchange markets. This was done in anticipation of a strengthening of the dollar, in which case the company would have earned enough profit to offset any unrealized loss resulting from foreign balance sheet translation. Unfortunately, the dollar fell and ITT lost $48 million, including $10 million in fees for the foreign contracts. Clearly, the use of foreign exchange markets to reduce balance sheet exposure placed management in a position of incurring actual cash costs and risks to protect bookkeeping results.

In addition, Serfass maintained that the recognition of translation gains and losses violates the "going concern" concept, a basic tenet of financial statement preparation, "in the respect that it forces a P&L effect on the translation process which is not caused by operational transactions."[36] The "P&L effect" cited by Serfass probably referred to translated and consolidated operating statements that would be valid if, and only if, the foreign operations had been conducted in the United States, in accordance with United States GAAP and tax regulations, and in United States dollars.

Violation of the "going concern" concept refers to translated and consolidated balance sheets that would be valid if, and only if, all foreign operations had been liquidated at the balance sheet date (without any losses or gains), the proceeds were remitted to the United States parent, the parent incurred conversion gains or losses only on conversions of the proceeds from the original foreign monetary items, and the parent duplicated the original foreign operations intact in the United States.

E. M. de Windt also found problems with *Statement No. 8*. He explained that the way in which rules on translating foreign currency could "transform a solid and profitable international operation into a big loser in dollars"[37] mystified him. He also found it difficult to believe that "the value of a 15-year foreign obligation could easily be revalued some 59 times before it has any real impact on the business."[38]

Not all of the articles published were unfavorable to *Statement No. 8*. In 1977, an article by Rita M. Rodriguez summarized the results of her study of the impact on the reported earnings for 1974 and 1975 of seventy United States multinationals included in the Fortune 500. The companies were selected on the basis of their large foreign direct investments in Europe, Japan, and Canada. She reported that "fewer than one-third of the companies in this sample found that *FASB No. 8* had a significant impact on their reported earnings."[39] Based on these results she concluded that "the adoption of *FASB No. 8* does not appear to have produced a major change in the earnings reported by most U.S. multinationals."[40]

William J. Bruns also provided support for the Statement, noting that it had eliminated the diversity in accounting practices in the area, a benefit with which most critics of the Statement were in agreement.[41] However, it was also cited that standardization was achieved at the expense of meeting the needs of financial statement users.[42] (In light of this criticism, the question naturally arises as to whether standardization was worth the cost.)

Secondly, Bruns maintained that "*FASB 8* drew attention to the strategic dimensions of managing and financing multinational enterprises . . . [and] enhanced the interest of top level managers in development of strategies for financing and controlling multinational operations."[43] (This may be true. However, the more pertinent questions are to what ends has such activity been directed and has this development been beneficial or detrimental to multinational corporations in general.)

In a preliminary study published in 1977 on the economic impact of FASB *Statement No. 8*, Murray J. Bryant and John K. Shank observed that the objective of the statement emphasized generally accepted accounting principles at the expense of economic substance.[44] Further, they pointed out that Rodriguez ignored a "key intervening variable which should be considered. That is, have the published results already been affected by changed management behavior?"[45] In their study, Bryant and Shank found evidence of a change in management behavior but no evidence of a change in stock market behavior. This led them to question the efficient market hypothesis and cite the need for more in-depth study.

A number of subsequent studies examined both management and market behavior. In 1978, Kerry Cooper, Donald R. Fraser, and R. Malcolm Richards published the results of their questionnaire survey of financial executives.[46] The questionnaire dealt with "the changes in management practices or procedures that firms might have employed to counter the potential adverse effects of *SFAS #8* on their financial statements."[47] The authors explained that if the requirements of *Statement No. 8* "trigger economic maneuvers which result in costs without corresponding benefits to the firm, it is possible that they are ill-conceived in terms of their contribution to economic decision-making and resource allocation."[48]

The results of this study pointed out a serious potential problem regarding the behavioral impact of the statement. Approximately half of the respondents reported "significant changes in management practices and procedures regarding foreign operations as the result of *SFAS #8*. A significant number reported an impact on capital investment decisions involving foreign operations."[49] Eighty-seven of the 195 firms responding to the survey reported changing management practices or procedures as a result of *Statement No. 8*. Of these, forty firms indicated that they increased hedging in foreign currency futures markets. This measure is not only expensive, but risky as well. Other measures taken in response to *Statement No. 8* included: refinancing debt in another currency (this often resulted in paying higher interest rates over the long-term to hedge an accounting exposure that might only exist in the short-term); increasing or decreasing cash remittances from foreign subsidiaries to the United States parent (this altered the subjections of foreign earnings to United States taxes); adjustments in average payment and collection periods of accounts denominated in a foreign currency; increased or decreased borrowing in a foreign currency; a change in the amount of local currency and marketable securities held in conjunction with foreign operations; and a change in the amount of accounts receivable denominated in a foreign currency. While it was possible that some of these changes had positive effects, it was certain that they all involved costs. "To the extent that these changes resulted in no cash flow benefit to the firm, and only reduced accounting (and not economic) exposure to foreign exchange risk — then any corresponding costs constitute a waste of firm resources."[50] This constituted a serious flaw in the statement, since, as the authors pointed out, consistency with generally accepted accounting principles alone was not sufficient justification. Accounting principles also should be behaviorally and economically sound. It was their consensus that *Statement No. 8* did not meet these criteria since the results of their study suggested that the statement led to management actions which were counter to the effective utilization of the firm's resources.

In 1979, Marjorie Stanley and Stanley B. Block also conducted a survey of multinational corporations. Their study indicated that financial officers did not consider *Statement No. 8* to be an improvement on the translation methods which they had previously used, and felt that it should be modified, particularly the prohibition of foreign exchange reserve accounts. In addition, the respondents appeared "hesitant to accept efficient market concepts"[51] with their perceptions often differing from those which they attributed to security analysts and investors. As a result, in attempts to protect their reported earnings positions, managements often took defensive measures which were noneconomic.[52] Despite such defensive measures, the volatility of reported earnings increased. Much of the volatility was found to stem from the translation of inventories and long-term debt. It was further noted that the treatment of these items had adverse effects on the *quality* of translated earnings. Therefore, the analyst and the investor needed a great deal of detailed information in order to arrive at informed judgments about the overall effect of the standard upon the reported earnings of the multinational corporation.[53] Unfortunately, due to the weak disclosure requirements of the statement, such detail was seldom, if ever, provided.

Further evidence of the Statement's effect on management and investor behavior was provided by John K. Shank, Jesse F. Dillard, and Richard J. Murdock.[54] In examining management behavior, they found:

1. The statement had a major impact on the choice of currencies in which debt was denominated:
    a. Fifty-two percent of the firms changed the mix between local currency debt and United States dollar debt in their capital structures to reduce their exposure to translation adjustments under *Statement No. 8*.
    b. Thirty-two percent of the firms believed that cash borrowing costs were significantly higher than they otherwise would have been because of the refinancings designed to avoid translation exposures under *Statement No. 8*. The extra interest was not readily visible, but the translation adjustments would have been.

2. *Statement No. 8* also affected the involvement of the firms in
   forward exchange markets:
   a. Sixty-eight percent of the firms at least sometimes entered the
      forward markets to cover translation exposures. While the
      authors did not specifically say this was a new development,
      the context in which it was reported indicated that it was a
      reaction to *Statement No. 8*.
   b. Sixteen percent of the firms believed they were being forced by
      earnings-per-share pressures to consider active hedging of
      translation exposures even though they had not done so yet.

3. The statement clearly had an impact on the internal reporting and
   control systems in the firms included in the study. Seventy-two
   percent of the firms indicated that their internal reporting systems
   changed significantly as a result of *Statement No. 8*. However, it
   was not specified how they changed.

4. Fifty-two percent of the firms indicated that they increased their
   use of outside consultants, at least partially, as a result of *Statement No. 8*. The type of consultants used was not mentioned, but
   it is likely that they were in the area of foreign exchange exposure
   management.

5. At least eighty percent of the firms said that *Statement No. 8* had
   significantly increased the amount of management time and attention devoted to foreign currency accounting. There was a consensus that, in light of the increased operating costs and the opportunity cost of management time diverted from other responsibilities,
   Statement No. 8 had an overall negative financial impact.[55]

In examining the effect of investor behavior on the capital markets as a
result of *Statement No. 8*, Shank, Dillard, and Murdock found

> no justification for changed management actions after *Statement No. 8* in terms of
> protecting shareholder returns; although the market did react negatively to the multina-
> tional firms in the 1975–77 period, it did not react more negatively to those firms affected
> by the *Statement*.[56]

Based on the results of their study, the authors concluded that
"accounting should reflect the economic substance of the underlying financial situation, if it is practical and feasible. At the very least, accounting
should not distort economic substance."[57] They went on to explain that if a
set of accounting requirements could be shown to distort economic reality
and induce uneconomic behavior, while an alternative set of more practical

accounting procedures could be adopted, the justification for the required rules becomes questionable. (That is what eventually led to the downfall of *Statement No. 8.*)

Philip M.J. Reckers and Martin E. Taylor also examined some of the alleged distortions created by the statement, and pointed out that the provisions of the statement were often inequitable and not representative of economic reality. Among their criticisms they noted that "by ignoring the economic hedge effected through foreign investment of debt proceeds, the prescriptions of *Statement No. 8* actually require the reporting of foreign currency gains or losses which seem to directly contradict reality."[58] As examples of economic hedges which were not regarded as hedges for accounting purposes, Reckers and Taylor mentioned the purchase of regulated utility property, the purchase of leased property that is fully contracted, or the issuance of walkaway debt. The authors concluded that *Statement No. 8* produced results that so grossly misrepresented the true earnings of foreign subsidiaries as to be positively misleading. While it was acknowledged that the Statement allowed the reporting entity to explain the fact that the reported results did not reflect the true economic results, the authors stressed that "it seems the objective of good financial reporting should be to have the financial statements reflect the true economic situation, not to explain in a footnote why the statements do not."[59] Such distortions led Reckers and Taylor to fear that *Statement No. 8* would motivate managers and stockholders to pursue suboptimal policies.

In addition to the foregoing, the effects of *Statement No. 8* have further complicated (if not obfuscated) the analysis of published financial statements.

The Impact of FASB *Statement No. 8* on Financial Statement Analysis

In 1976, Leopold A. Bernstein noted that *Statement No. 8* had some major implications for financial analysts. Aside from its effect on income, the Statement also affected such important financial position relationships as the current ratio, the acid test ratio, and debt-equity ratios as well as performance in areas such as return on investment.[60] Bernstein's observations concerning ratios are valid only with respect to return on investment, since ROI (return on investment) is affected by changes in income and, more importantly, since ROI is a useful macromeasure. Where *consolidated* statements are concerned, the other ratios mentioned are blunt, if not misleading, tools. Current and acid-test ratios assume that the consolidated resources reported are available *ratably* to cover consolidated liabilities whereas they are not, of course. Consolidated debt-equity ratios are similarly flawed since the consolidation process aggregates and reports all but intercompany debt while eliminating all subsidiary equity attributed to the parent. It may well be that, as a result of observations such as those above, examinations of the effects of *Statement No. 8* and similar pronouncements will lead to realization of the limited usefulness of consolidated reports, as the primary statements, and greater emphasis upon more meaningful non-aggregated reportings.

Bernstein also discussed other implications of the Statement upon such items as: (1) capital structure considerations, (2) inventory valuations, and (3) depreciation and amortization factors.

In discussing capital structure considerations, Bernstein noted that the capital structure and the composition of assets and liabilities of companies took on increased importance for the financial analyst. He explained that, under *Statement No. 8*, a foreign subsidiary highly levered in foreign debt was less affected by changes in exchange rates than was a foreign subsidiary financed mainly with equity or United States dollar debt. However, what Bernstein failed to mention was that in most cases this information would not be available to the analyst.

Concerning inventory valuations, Bernstein observed that translating inventories at historical rates often resulted in a company with large inventories (and a short foreign exchange position) showing a translation gain on the devaluation of foreign currency and a loss on the revaluation of the foreign currency. Conversely, a company with small inventories was likely to show a gain on revaluation and a loss on devaluation.

Bernstein also warned that, unlike most other revenue and expense items which were translated at the average exchange rate for the year, depreciation and amortization were translated using the historical rates attached to the related assets. Consequently, the distorting impact of translation on income statement items was magnified in relation to the significance of depreciation and amortization in the total income statement.

In addition, Bernstein discussed some of the controversial provisions of the statement. He noted that many people took issue with the provision that required inventories and fixed assets to be translated at historical rates while requiring the foreign debt incurred to finance them to be translated at the current rate. It was maintained that not only did this cause the translated results and relationships to differ significantly from those reflected in the foreign financial statements, but that it also could cause distortions and serious fluctuations in income which could be misinterpreted by investors. He also noted that there was some opposition to the current recognition of unrealized foreign exchange translation "gains" on the grounds that it was not in accord with conservative accounting principles.

Finally, Bernstein cautioned analysts to be aware that the fluctuation of currency rates was only one of the items influencing the impact of foreign operations on a company's financial statements. Other items which should be considered include: the location of assets and liabilities, inter-country transactions, foreign taxation trends, differing fiscal years of foreign entities, restrictions on remittances of funds, and the currencies in which sales are effected.[61]

Two years later, in 1978, William C. Norby noted the lack of adequate disclosure requirements in *Statement No. 8*. At that time, Norby high-lighted three main criticisms of the Statement. First, it did not specify a format for reporting foreign currency translation gains and losses. Therefore, due to the all-inclusive income approach, these items were often lumped together with operating income despite the fact that they were largely unrealized and represented nonoperating gains and losses. Second, the statement did not require separate reporting of the effects of translation on current operations. Thus, the financial statement user was hard pressed to find the effect of this factor on reported earnings. Third, the statement prescribed an accounting method that often failed to portray the firm's true economic position in foreign-currency-denominated assets. Therefore, due to the complexity of foreign currency translation accounting, Norby stated that the Financial Analysts Federation's Financial Accounting Policy Committee "believes investor understanding would be enhanced if the presentation format were standardized, including an explanatory note that shows the effects of foreign currency translation on both operations and the balance sheet."[62]

Managing and Controlling the Accounting and/or Economic Risk of Exchange Rate Changes

In December 1976, *Business Week* noted that banks had experienced increases in foreign exchange trade and in the demand for their advisory services in the area of foreign exchange. In fact, Gerald Kramer, vice-president for corporate foreign exchange and risk management systems at Chase Manhattan Bank, remarked that they could not have devised a better marketing tool for their foreign exchange consulting services than FASB *Statement No. 8*.[63]

Kramer explained that, over time, hedging was a zero-sum game in which the costs of hedging equalled the losses that would have been incurred without it. He also cautioned that, unless properly timed, hedgings of large amounts of a foreign currency often tended to bring about the very events the hedgings sought to offset.

Business Week again touched on this topic in 1977 when it discussed the growing popularity of the long-term currency swap as a means of achieving long-term financing in soft currency countries and hedging against losses from fluctuations in foreign exchange rates.[64] Most long-term currency swaps took place between United States and British multinational corporations, with the United States firm offering dollars in exchange for British sterling. The two companies would agree to exchange a given amount of the two currencies for a period of approximately ten years (this time period would vary depending on the needs of the companies involved). At the end of the agreed upon time period, the money was re-exchanged. In order to offset the higher cost of borrowing in Britain, the United States company would pay a single premium fee for the exchange agreement.

In his 1978 article, Alan Teck defined four types of foreign exchange exposure for a typical multinational: translation, transaction, historical, and opportunity. According to Teck's definition:

1. *Translation exposure* involved assets or liabilities carried at current prices and translated at current exchange rates. If exchange rates on the day of translation differed from those previously used for translation, *Statement No. 8* required the recognition of an "exchange gain or loss." Therefore, these assets were considered "exposed."

2. *Transaction exposure* involved receipts or payments measured or denominated in a currency other than the one used by the reporting entity. *Statement No. 8* required that any change in the exchange rate between the transaction date and the settlement date be accounted for as an "exchange gain or loss." Therefore, the transaction was considered exposed.

3. *Historical exposure* involved assets recorded in the financial statements at historic prices and translated at historic exchange rates. *Statement No. 8* assumed that for such assets any change in exchange rates would either be offset by increased revenue or would be reflected in higher asset values. If neither was possible historical exposure existed.

4. *Opportunity exposure* involved opportunities for realizing exchange gains or losses because a company had commitments for future transactions denominated in a foreign currency that were not yet recorded in the financial statements.

He indicated that while FASB *Statement No. 8* recognized only translation and transaction exposures, the largest exchange problems typically fell into the historical exposure or the opportunity exposure category. Therefore, he reasoned that the question of when to hedge had no simple answer.

In most situations, difficult judgments must be made about the desirability of obtaining protection after considering the cost of hedging, the risk of additional cash losses related to the hedge and the likely impact of translation losses on the company's activities and cost of capital.[65]

In his 1979 study of currency strategies under *Statement No. 8*, Paul Munter performed empirical tests dealing with two main issues. The first was the change in currency strategies for foreign subsidiaries aimed at minimizing the effect of *Statement No. 8* on the consolidated financial statements. The second was the use of different strategies for foreign subsidiaries in strong currency countries than for foreign subsidiaries in weak currency countries. Munter's tests revealed that the following strategies were utilized: changing the relationship between fixed assets and total liabilities, changing the relationship between monetary assets and monetary liabilities, replacing debt in stronger currencies with debt in weaker currencies, increasing dividend payments from foreign subsidiaries, and reducing the outstanding debt of foreign subsidiaries.

Munter also found that multinational corporations with foreign subsidiaries in strong currency countries were reacting differently to the statement than were those with foreign subsidiaries in weak currency countries. However, he noted that the difference appeared to be more one of magnitude than of direction. Munter speculated that this was due to the fact that when a foreign currency strengthened against the United States dollar, firms with subsidiaries in that country were more likely to report a translation loss than a translation gain. On the other hand, when a foreign currency weakened against the United States dollar, firms with foreign subsidiaries in that country were more likely to report a translation gain. Therefore, he reasoned that firms with subsidiaries in strong currency countries were primarily interested in avoiding the consequences of the statement.[66]

In another examination of foreign exchange exposure management, James T. Sherwin noted that, in developing an approach to the problem, "financial management must first define what foreign exchange exposure needs protection."[67] He listed three basic possibilities: (1) Total profit and loss exposure coverage, consisting of balance sheet translations and transactional cash flows; (2) Transactional exposure coverage only, involving payables and receivables denominated in nonlocal currencies; (3) No coverage.

Sherwin concluded that, "Once this policy decision is reached, each multinational can apply its own solution to its own currency risk position."[68]

Gaffney Feskoe took a similar position stating that, prior to engaging in any activities aimed at eliminating foreign exchange risk, a corporation should first determine its exposure, define its attitude toward risk, and formulate a corporate foreign exchange management policy. Among other things, such a policy should specify whether accounting or economic exposure was more important to the company, who was responsible for implementing the exposure policy, and the limits that must be adhered to in managing the exposure risk. The next step would be to develop a currency forecast in order to define the risk of future exposure. Once a forecast was chosen for management purposes, the corporation could then select from a number of hedging vehicles available for managing its exposures. Those hedging strategies might include:

1. Forward exchange contracts;

2. Local currency borrowing;

3. Leading and lagging (speeding up or delaying payment on payables denominated in a foreign currency in order to hedge against the appreciation or depreciation, respectively, of the foreign currency);

4. Cash management;

5. Parallel loans (two independent corporations, which have a mutual long-term need for the other's home currency, exchange currencies, creating a liability to offset an exposed asset position);

6. Parallel hedges (a company, which has foreign subsidiaries in two countries whose currencies are closely linked, is long in one currency and short in the other—the net liability position in one currency acts as a hedge for the net asset position in the other);

7. Simulated dollar loans (where a foreign currency is difficult or impossible to remit, a cash-rich subsidiary of one company lends money to a cash-poor subsidiary of another and the parent of the cash-poor subsidiary agrees to compensate, in dollars, the parent of the cash-rich subsidiary for any exchange loss on the amount of the loan);

8. Raising local prices in a country of depreciating currency.

Therefore, Feskoe concluded, while it is

impossible to overcome the uncertainty of the exchange markets, it is possible to plan strategies for dealing with uncertainty. By isolating the exposures a company may have, and by planning in advance the methods that will be used to deal with these exposures—through a formal corporate policy—some of the worry can be eliminated in confronting a volatile marketplace.[69]

FASB *Statement No. 52* **and Related Topics**

The reaction to the adoption of FASB *Statement No. 52* has been varied. While some see it as an improvement over *Statement No. 8*, others do not. Either way, *Statement No. 52* does have its problems — as indicated by the slim four-to-three margin of acceptance it received from FASB members. Some executives have questioned the wisdom of releasing such an important standard on the basis of this weak passage, observing that rules passed by the APB under similarly narrow margins were later changed.[70]

During the exposure draft stage, Clifford Grease, a partner at Peat, Marwick, Mitchell and Co., concluded that *Statement No. 8* was the most controversial and unpopular opinion the FASB produced and that the new statement was likely to be the second. Others argued that there simply was no best way to account for foreign currency fluctuations.[71]

Arlene Hershman noted that many companies which favored the changes made by *Statement No. 52* still had trouble with some of its provisions. Some complained about distorting effects when the statement was applied to companies with subsidiaries in countries where the currency had been experiencing inflation rates much higher or lower than the U.S. dollar. Others objected to the fact that translation gains generally were not to be reflected in income until the investment in the foreign subsidiary was liquidated or sold. They claimed that a company could have "a steadily growing equity account resulting from the increasing value of its overseas assets, but this progress would never show up in earnings reports to stockholders."[72] (This criticism, while understandable, is not entirely justified. In fact, the recognition of such translation "gains and losses" in income was one of the criticisms of *Statement No. 8* that *Statement No. 52* was intended to correct.)

Gerald White of the Financial Analysts Federation took the position that investors were interested in projecting future cash flows and the results of operations in United States dollars, not in a foreign currency. He believed that the new statement did not provide the information needed for such an analysis.[73]

In a slightly different vein, Allan Lyons, accounting analyst for Value Line's Investment Survey, observed that as a result of the new statement, analysts would have to "learn to work with two numbers, not just earnings per share."[74] These numbers were operating income in the form of earnings per share and book value per share. (This observation is somewhat misguided in that analysts should examine a myriad of factors concerning the corporation and not simply rely on one or two factors in their analyses.) Recognizing this fact, Norman Weinger, accounting analyst for Wall Street's Oppenheimer and Co., observed that the new statement would not necessarily make financial analysis any easier. Even though earnings performance might be more predictable, according to Weinger, the book value would become a "meaningless number" and earnings swings would be replaced by a "bouncing balance sheet" (swings in book value).[75]

Prior to the issuance of the new statement, Hershman cautioned the FASB against a resolution that would make it more difficult for investors to compare performances, because "the needs of the users of financial reports is a prime consideration in rule making."[76] Unfortunately, added user difficulty is what some fear *Statement No. 52* will produce. "Several dislike the idea of 'burying' the translation adjustment on the grounds that users of annual reports will be confused by the effect of foreign currency exposure on the company's worth."[77]

The principal criticism of the National Association of Accountants' Management Accounting Practices Committee (MAP) regarding the new statement concerned the erosion of the "clean surplus" doctrine—which refers to the requirement that translation gains and losses be accumulated and carried as a component of stockholders equity without being shown on the income statement. Those items excluded from the income statement include:

1. Translation adjustments ("gains and losses") resulting from the process of translating a foreign entity's financial statements from the functional currency to United States dollars (until the sale or until the complete or substantially complete liquidation of the net investment in the foreign entity).

2. Transaction gains and losses (results of the effect of exchange rate changes on transactions denominated in currencies other than the functional currency) where the transaction hedges a foreign currency commitment or a net investment in a foreign entity.

3. Transaction gains and losses attributable to intercompany foreign currency transactions that are of a long-term investment nature.

MAP argued that these gains and losses contain both realized and unrealized portions and that the realized portions should be shown on the income statement. While they agreed that the unrealized portions should be deferred, they held that it should be as "balance sheet deferred credits or charges and not as elements of stockholders equity."[78]

Others complained that "the immediate transaction impact of holding foreign currency debt, including dollar debt on a foreign subsidiary's books, will limit (multinational corporations') flexibility in choosing financing alternatives. In order to eliminate transaction adjustments on the income statement resulting from the debt, foreign subsidiaries will apparently be encouraged to borrow locally in their own currencies for their own needs."[79] On the positive side, the above could help to strengthen the United States dollar by slowing its flow overseas and, thereby, aid in slowing the rate of inflation in the United States.[80] There could also be a negative impact if corporations planned their debt financing based on where the related translation or transaction gains and losses would appear — in the balance sheet or income statement.

Another potential problem with the new statement was noted by Norlin G. Rueschoff and Leonard M. Savoie. They pointed out that while the statement did not permit a choice of translation methods, it did permit the choice of functional currency. Therefore, companies in certain situations might choose a functional currency on the basis of the translation method afforded and the results which it would produce.[81]

Rueschoff and Savoie also noted that business enterprises "operating and reporting in the international environment must provide financial statements that are useful to investors."[82] One of the ways in which *Statement No. 52* tried to do this was by distinguishing between two types of currency effect — "transaction gains or losses, which have an immediate impact on a firm's 'cash flow'; and translation effects stemming from a company's capital investment in foreign countries, but where typically no cash is involved right away."[83]

It has been said that, by requiring translation gains and losses to be reflected in a separate section of stockholders' equity on the balance sheet instead of in income, the new statement should provide a

> twofold advantage with respect to United States multinational corporations: (1) remove the unpredictable "gyrating" effect on reported earnings and (2) assist investors in a better understanding of reported earnings, since earnings from foreign subsidiaries should be more predictable than they were under *SFAS No. 8*.[84]

There are several problems with the above opinion. First of all, if the functional currency of the foreign subsidiary is deemed to be the United States dollar, or if the subsidiary is located in a country that is deemed to have a highly inflationary economy, translation gains and losses will continue to be recognized in income instead of being reflected in stockholders' equity. Therefore, some companies may still experience a yo-yo effect on earnings.

Secondly, where foreign currencies are functional, companies may find that earnings swings have been replaced by "bouncing balance sheets." The new sections of stockholders' equity may also confuse some financial statement users who will not understand what the unfamiliar numbers represent.

Another point of confusion may involve the two methods of translation that are now allowed. Without a requirement for disclosure of which method was used in a given situation, financial statement users could become confused as to how the results were derived and as to what the results represented. For example, assume that the United States based parent (P) has a foreign subsidiary (SA) which in turn has a foreign subsidiary (SB) of its own and the functional currency of both SA and SB is determined to be the local currency of SA. Then the financial statements of SA and SB will be consolidated using the temporal method of translation. These results will then be consolidated with the parent's results using the current rate method of translation. Another example concerns a parent that has two foreign subsidiaries, SC and SD, and the functional currency of SC is the local currency while the functional currency of SD is the United States dollar. Then the financial statements of SC will be translated using the current rate method and the financial statement of SD will be translated using the temporal method.

Criticism was also leveled at *Statement No. 52* by the three dissenting board members. They indicated that they could not support the new statement because it:

1. Builds on two incompatible premises and, as a result, produces anomalies and a significant but unwarranted reporting distinction between transaction gains and losses and translation adjustments. (The first premise is that it is the parent company's net investment in a foreign operation, rather than the foreign operation's individual assets and liabilities, that is subject to exchange rate risk. The second premise is that the translation process should retain the relationships in foreign currency financial statements as measured by the functional currency.)

2. Adopts objectives and methods that are at variance with fundamental concepts that underlie present financial reporting. (This criticism refers to the objectives of translation set forth in the Statement to: (a) provide information that is generally compatible with the expected economic effects of a rate change, and (b) reflect the financial results and relationships of foreign operations as measured in their functional currencies in conformity with United States generally accepted accounting principles. It also refers to the methods of translation prescribed: (i) the current rate method which requires the use of an accumulated translation adjustment in stockholders' equity and (ii) the temporal method. The dissenters argue that the Statement challenges and rejects the dollar perspec-

tive underlying the existing theories of historical cost and capital maintenance, inflation accounting, consolidation, and realization.)

3. Incorrectly assumes that an aggregation of the results of foreign operations measured in functional currencies and expressed in dollars, rather than consolidated results measured in dollars, assists United States investors and creditors in assessing future cash flows.

4. Will not result in similar accounting for similar circumstances. (For example, the dissenters believe the criteria for deciding whether to use the current rate or the temporal method of translation are inappropriate and that the application of these criteria will not necessarily result in the same method of translation being used in similar situations. Likewise, they believe the absence of effective criteria that would objectively determine when foreign currency transactions and foreign exchange contracts are hedges may result in transaction gains and losses being reported as translation adjustments or deferred as hedge commitments, when they should be reported currently in net income. The dissenters also object to the variety of permissible methods of translation from existing *Statement No. 8* requirements.)[85]

For the most part, their criticisms do have some validity. The Statement does build on two incompatible premises. The first premise of the parent company's net investment in a foreign operation being subject to exchange risk reflects a dollar perspective of exchange rate risk. Thus, it calls for a dollar measure of the effects of exchange rate changes. The second premise of retaining the measurement relationships in functional currency financial statements calls for a functional currency measure of the effects of exchange rate changes. It is also true that the functional currency approach taken by the Statement rejects the dollar perspective that underlies existing accounting theory. However, it must be remembered that this statement is addressing a question of global proportions. Therefore, it should adopt a global perspective. In a multinational environment, it can no longer be assumed that the only items of importance are the dollar results. There are a variety of reasons for a company to invest overseas (tax advantages, governmental restrictions, etc.). The intent of financial reporting should be to highlight the reasons, not to ignore them. Nevertheless, it is true that the approach taken by the Statement is not the most useful approach for assisting investors and creditors in assessing the future cash flows they will receive. Finally, the dissenters are correct in their observations that the lack of specificity in the Statement's requirements may result in different approaches being used in similar circumstances.

However, the answer does not appear to lie in retention of *Statement No. 8.* To complete the perspective on the subject, it seems appropriate to review some of the *conceptual* issues underlying foreign currency translation and some of the alternatives that have been suggested over the years.

The Conceptual Issues Underlying Foreign Currency Accounting

Much of the foregoing has dealt with specific criticisms of specific accounting or reporting techniques. Admittedly, even the most tightly constructed review of comments and opinions expressed over most of a decade can easily overwhelm. Consequently, it is often beneficial to step back and examine the basic frameworks of the dilemmas. Both *Statement No. 8* and *Statement No. 52* were constructed by knowledgeable, well-intentioned groups of experts upon certain frameworks of objectives. Perhaps the objectives were faulty. Or, perhaps the Board attempted to do something that simply could not be accomplished.

Remittable Funds

In his discussion of theory underlying foreign currency translation, Joseph E. Connor asserted that

> once an investment is made in a foreign country it is there to stay, and the only meaningful information to an investor is the statistical notation of the current dollar equivalent of the total of such investment and its current earnings. . . . Under this theory, the only real foreign earnings are those which can be remitted. When remittable profits become the goal or governing limitation, the use of any translation rates other than current rates is obviously improper. Remittable profits will be determined in local currency and dollar equivalent at current or negotiated remittance rates.[86]

Connor also noted that the earnings of foreign operations are measured by local currency sales and costs. Therefore, the use of current rates in the translation process would improve the fairness of the income statement and preserve the important operating relationships that exist.[87]

Future Earnings Streams

Lee J. Seidler took a different approach, proposing that an appropriate goal for the translation process would be "the valuation of the future stream of earnings to be received from the foreign subsidiary, in terms of the currency of the parent company."[88] He explained that in the late 1960s,

American accountants began to recognize the increased preoccupation of the American financial markets with reported earnings. This led them to shift their attention away from balance sheet presentations and toward the reportings of incomes. With these apparent trends, Seidler continued, "it seems clearly out of date for translation accounting to be concerned merely with the recreation or fictional establishment (in the case of foreign assets actually purchased with foreign currencies) of a largely outdated original cost figure."[89] Seidler concluded that the translation process should not attempt to eliminate foreign operations, but should represent them as viable units apart from their parents.

His method called for the use of an earning power criterion to determine whether to translate at current rates or at historic rates, depending on the anticipated effect on future earnings streams. Where the dollar values of future earnings streams from the sale or use of physical assets were expected to remain relatively constant, Seidler suggested the use of historic rates. Where the dollar values of future earnings streams were expected to change, Seidler suggested the use of current rates. He reasoned that, in accordance with the contemporary emphasis of valuing an investment based on future earnings streams, it made sense to select a translation method that would attempt to measure the effects of changes in exchange rates on the dollar values of future earnings streams from the foreign subsidiary.

Seidler also criticized the use of the average exchange rate to translate income statement items. He argued that the balance sheet and income statement should be in similar dollars and that the profit shown should be that which resulted from the transactions in terms of end-of-the-year dollars. According to Seidler, "income statements translated entirely at the closing exchange rate would seem to present a more reasonable picture of earning capacity, on the basis of the most currently available information."[90]

Basic Disclosures

Unlike Connor and Seidler, Edgar M. Barrett and Leslie L. Spero did not argue for a particular method of translation. Instead, they emphasized the need for financial statement users to know at least three major factors in order to appraise intelligently the consolidated statements of a multinational enterprise: The accounting method used for translating the financial statements of the foreign subsidiary from the foreign currency; the composition of the foreign subsidiary's balance sheet (particularly the composition of its working capital and its capital structure, which can effect the amount of the translation gain or loss recognized); and the timing of the recognition of the resulting translation gain or loss.[91] Neither *Statement No. 8* nor *No. 52* required the disclosure of this basic information.

Situational Reportings

In 1976, John K. Shank warned that caution should be used in interpreting annual reports prepared under *Statement No. 8* because, in his opinion, the statement represented a "forthright, firm, and unequivocal step in the wrong direction."[92] He reasoned that the appropriateness of recognizing "exchange gains and losses" in income depended on the nature of the gains and losses involved. However, the Statement made no distinction between exchange "gains and losses" resulting from closed exchanges, open exchanges, or the translation of foreign financial statements. Shank also complained that, by equating economic exposure to net monetary position, the Statement made a gross oversimplification. As a result, the accounting treatment of translation gains and losses did not necessarily measure the correct magnitude nor direction of the economic gain or loss.[93]

Thomas G. Evans discussed this area in more detail, distinguishing between pure economic exposure and "earnings per share" exposure. He explained that, in the purest economic sense, exposure exists when a person or firm has a receivable or debt denominated in a foreign currency that is allowed to fluctuate against the domestic currency. In this case, exposure is the risk that the relative values of the currencies will change between the time the transaction is initiated and concluded. As such, Evans concluded that two main features of exposure are that only a direct party to the transaction is exposed and conversion must take place or be intended. In addition, he maintained that *Statement No. 8* failed to recognize this by defining the "exposed position" of the foreign subsidiary as the net monetary position.

Therefore, Evans suggested that "from the viewpoint of the rules on currency translation, a new kind of exposure needs to be recognized, 'earnings per share' exposure."[94] This refers to the fact that recognizing translation gains and losses in income (as required by the statement) had a direct impact on earnings per share and often resulted in management feeling pressured to take steps to minimize such losses. Unfortunately, those steps frequently included the use of foreign exchange contracts and other measures which increased economic exposure.[95]

In 1978, Ronald M. Copeland and Robert W. Ingram reviewed the theoretical basis for the recognition of unrealized gains and losses specified in *Statement No. 8*. They examined three alternative ways of accounting for unrealized translation gains and losses: nonrecognition of interim events, immediate recognition of unrealized gains or losses, or, deferred recognition of unrealized interim gains or losses.

Based on the results of their study, they concluded that the deferral of interim translation gains and losses was the most satisfactory choice, since it was the only suggested alternative "capable of producing both the best approximation of the liquidation values of exchange transactions and the least distortion in firms' earnings performances."[96] As such, it was deemed to be the only method which met the primary objectives of both the asset/liability view (by recognizing unrealized gains and losses to preserve the integrity of the balance sheet) and the revenue/expense view (by deferring unrealized gains and losses to avoid distortion of periodic earnings) of conceptual theory.[97]

Eclectic Disclosures

When, in 1979, the FASB added the amendment of *Statement No. 8* to its agenda, Shank and Gary S. Shamis cited the inadequacy of the statement's disclosure requirements. They pointed out that generally accepted accounting principles required that "disclosures be adequate to ensure a full and fair presentation of the financial situation"[98] and questioned how the statement could remotely be considered to meet this standard when "the users of the financial statements must interpret the impact of exchange rate adjustments based on a single line item."[99] In order to remedy this situation, they recommended that the FASB "broaden the scope of the specific disclosure requirements regarding foreign currency adjustments."[100] They suggested the following:

1. A breakdown of the foreign exchange adjustment into the categories of realized transaction gains or losses, unrealized transaction-based gains or losses, and translation gains or losses

2. A break out of the foreign exchange adjustment by major currencies, and

3. Additional income statement disclosures indicating the impact of exchange rate changes on specific income statement amounts.

The authors believed that additional disclosures such as those suggested above would enhance the usefulness of the accounting data by enabling intelligent interpretations of the exchange adjustments.[101]

Unfortunately, the FASB did not include such disclosure rules in *Statement No. 52*.

Summary Observations

Statement No. 8 had some positive effects. It standardized foreign currency translation by reducing the diversity of translation, reporting, and disclo-

Figure 1.   Advantages of FASB *Statement No. 8*

---

1. FASB-8 increased the comparability of multinational financial statements by reducing the diversity of translation, reporting, and disclosure practices.

2. FASB-8 highlighted the strategic dimensions of managing and financing multinational enterprises.

3. Proponents contended that the erratic swings in earnings produced by FASB-8 merely reflected the risks inherent in international operations under a system of floating exchange rates.

4. Proponents liked the fact that FASB-8 looked at foreign currency translation from a dollar perspective.

---

sure practices. It also resulted in senior management devoting more time and attention to foreign-exchange risks (see fig. 1).

Unfortunately, the shortcomings of *Statement No. 8* outweighed the benefits. Chief among these shortcomings was the distorting "yo-yo" effect on reported earnings which resulted. The Statement's problems were further exacerbated by its weak disclosure requirements (see fig. 2).

Statement No. 52 made certain improvements in foreign currency translation. It reduced the "yo-yo" effect on earnings and operating margin distortions. It also resulted in more economically compatible results (see fig. 3).

A number of faults remained in *Statement No. 52*. Where the reporting currency was the functional currency or where the foreign operations were located in a highly inflationary economy, the problems that existed under *Statement No. 8* were still present. The faults persisted because the method of translation prescribed was essentially the same as the *Statement No. 8* method. Where the foreign currency was the functional currency, new problems were introduced, such as earnings swings being replaced by "bouncing balance sheets." There also had been concern expressed that *Statement No. 52* rejected the dollar perspective in favor of a functional currency perspective and that it violated the clean surplus doctrine. As in the case of *Statement No. 8*, the problems of *Statement No. 52* were complicated by weak disclosure requirements (see fig. 4).

Figure 2.   Disadvantages of FASB *Statement No. 8*

---

1. The objective of FASB-8 was inadequate and improper.

2. FASB-8's procedures were conversion-oriented and ill-suited to present day multinational networks.

3. As a whole, FASB-8 violated the going concern concept.

4. FASB-8 effectively emphasized cash-basis accounting results over those of accrual accounting.

5. At times, FASB-8 distorted and adversely affected long-term investments, capital movements, and international trade.

6. FASB-8 affected important financial position relationships and performance in areas such as return on investment.

7. Under FASB-8 translation of inventory and foreign debt resulted in mismatching of costs and revenues.

8. FASB-8 resulted in misstated profit margins.

9. FASB-8 resulted in erratic swings in earnings (the "yo-yo" effect).
    a. This led to erratic and misleading interpretations of profit performance.
    b. The job of determining the quality of reported earnings was complicated.
    c. Forecasting future earnings was more difficult. The financial statement user had no firm basis on which to judge the company's results of operations.

10. FASB-8 distorted reality.
    a. It emphasized GAAP at the expense of economic substance.
    b. It resulted in some economically poor decisions being reported as economically good decisions in the external financial statements.

        c.   It prescribed an accounting method that often failed to portray the firm's true economic position in foreign-currency-denominated assets.

11.   FASB-8 affected the way multinationals conducted business.
        a.   It increased activity in international hedging and financing.
        b.   It resulted in management actions which were counter to the effective utilization of the firm's resources. Management often risked incurring economic (real) losses in an effort to hedge against translation (unreal or paper) losses.

12.   FASB-8 assumed that only monetary items were exposed to "exchange gains and losses."

13.   FASB-8 was self-contradictory in that it actually resulted in the revaluation of foreign assets and liabilities.

14.   FASB-8 did not distinguish between transaction and translation gains and losses.

15.   FASB-8 had very weak disclosure requirements.
        a.   Disclosures did not provide sufficient detail to allow analysts and investors to arrive at informed judgments about the overall effect of the statement on reported earnings.
        b.   It did not specify a format for reporting foreign currency translation gains and losses.
        c.   It did not require separate reporting of the effects of translation on current operations.

The demise of *Statement No. 8* demonstrated the apparent futility of applying normative (simplex) methods to situational (complex) issues. In designing the functional currency approach prescribed by *Statement No. 52*, the FASB moved toward a recognition of situational differences. Unfortunately, this move stopped short of what was needed.

Situational approaches mandate the isolation of criteria for defining

Figure 3. Advantages of FASB *Statement No. 52*

1. FASB-52 allowed for differences in foreign operations by adopting the functional currency approach
   which matched the method of translation to the
   situation.
       a. The current rate method of translation was
          designated where the foreign currency was
          the functional currency (except where for-
          eign operations were operating in highly
          inflationary environments).
       b. The temporal method of translation was
          designated where the reporting currency
          (United States dollar) was the functional
          currency.
       c. The temporal method of translation was
          also designated where the foreign entity
          was operating in a highly inflationary
          environment (defined as a three year
          cumulative inflation rate of approxi-
          mately 100 percent).

2. FASB-52's current rate method of translation resolved several problems that had existed under
   FASB-8:
       a. The problem of economically incompatible
          results.
       b. The problem of operating margin distor-
          tions.
       c. The problem of earnings volatility dis-
          tortions (by recording the translation
          adjustment directly to stockholders
          equity).

3. FASB-52 distinguished between transaction and
   translation gains and losses.

4. FASB-52 could help to strengthen the United States
   dollar and aid in slowing the rate of inflation in
   the United States by encouraging local currency
   financing (borrowing) and, thus, slowing the flow
   of the United States dollar overseas.

Figure 4. Disadvantages of FASB *Statement No. 52*

1. FASB-52 built on two incompatible premises.
    a. The parent company's net foreign invest-
        ment rather than the individual foreign
        assets and liabilities was exposed to ex-
        change rate risk.
    b. The translation process should retain the
        relationships in the foreign financial
        statements.

2. FASB-52 adopted objectives and methods which were
    at variance with the fundamental concepts under-
    lying financial reporting
    a. distorted the meaning of book value
    b. violated the "clean surplus" doctrine
    c. rejected the dollar perspective.

3. FASB-52 did not provide the information needed
    for projecting future dollar cash flows and the
    results of operations in United States dollars.

4. FASB-52 incorrectly assumed that consolidated re-
    sults measured in functional currencies rather
    than dollars would be more useful in assisting
    United States investors and creditors in assess-
    ing future cash flows.

5. FASB-52 did not result in similar accounting for
    similar circumstances in some cases.

6. FASB-52 resulted in distorting effects when ap-
    plied to companies with subsidiaries in countries
    experiencing inflation rates much higher or lower
    than the United States.

7. FASB-52 increased user difficulty by expanding
    the acceptable alternatives and complicating the
    translation process.
    a. It was more difficult to compare per-
        formance.
    b. Statement users could be confused as to
        how the translation numbers were derived.
    c. The new section of stockholder's equity
        could confuse statement users who did not
        understand what it represented.

Figure 4 (contd.)

---

8. FASB-52 could unduly influence financing deci-
    sions by encouraging local currency borrowing.

9. The choice of a functional currency was based on
    the results that would be produced. (This could
    entail changes in the way foreign operations con-
    duct business in order to meet the criteria.)

10. FASB-52 resulted in some companies using the tem-
    poral method of translation still experiencing a
    "yo-yo" (gyrating) effect on earnings.

11. FASB-52 resulted in some companies using the cur-
    rent rate method of translation finding earnings
    swings replaced by bouncing balance sheets.

12. FASB-52 had weak disclosure requirements.

---

situations and then selecting the most appropriate (fairest) reporting/
disclosure mechanisms. While *Statement No. 52* developed a set of criteria
for determining the functional currency of foreign operations, these criteria
were criticized as being inconclusive. Another problem was that once the
method of translation was selected, based on the functional currency, there
were no allowances for situational differences. In addition, the disclosure
requirements of the Statement proved to be vague and inadequate.

Accountants and statement issuers would be well-advised to recognize
and accept the fact that merely furnishing raw data is no longer acceptable
in these complex times. This point was accentuated clearly by Paul Kolton,
Chairman of the Financial Accounting Standards Advisory Council, when
he said,

> We are approaching a time—and may already be there—when virtually all the issues
> being tackled by the FASB are more complex and, in the minds of some observers, no
> fully satisfactory solutions are even possible. I would include in this category foreign
> currency translation.[102]

As indicated earlier, full and fair disclosures, accompanied by meaningful explanations, seem to be the only approach to achieving the objectives of FASB *SFA Concepts No. 1*. This would provide management with a
format in which to explain its situation—past, present, and future. It would
also clarify foreign currency translation for financial statement users,
allowing them to more intelligently interpret the information presented and
to make any adjustments which they deemed useful in their analysis.

5

Review of Current Reporting Practice

Introduction

In order to assess the adequacy of current reporting practice for the area of foreign currency translation, a survey of published financial statements was made. This chapter describes the sample selection, the methodology used, and the results of the survey study.

Sample Selection

The sample chosen consisted of the 1981 financial statements of the 100 largest United States multinationals listed in the July 5, 1982 issue of *Forbes*. The list of firms is shown in Table 2. This was not intended to be a random sample but rather a representative group of firms which were likely to be affected by foreign currency translation.

Methodology

The next step in the review process was to examine the financial statements of the sample companies in order to determine the following:

1. Did the company use *Statement No. 8* or *Statement No. 52*?

2. Were the minimum reporting requirements, as specified by the applicable statement, met?

3. Did the company merely conform to the minimum requirements or did it go beyond the minimum in order to provide more informative disclosure in keeping with the spirit and intent of the pronouncements?

4. Was the reported information displayed in a manner that highlighted its importance or was it obscured?

Table 2.   100 Largest United States Multinational Firms

1.   Exxon

2.   Mobil

3.   Texaco

4.   Standard Oil Calif.

5.   Ford Motor

6.   General Motors

7.   IBM

8.   Phibro-Salomon

9.   Citicorp

10.   International Telephone and Telegraph

11.   Gulf Oil

12.   Bank America

13.   Chase Manhattan

14.   E. I. Du Pont de Nemours

15.   General Electric

16.   Dow Chemical

17.   Standard Oil of Indiana

18.   Occidental Petroleum

19.   J. P. Morgan

20.   Safeway Stores

21.   Sun Company

22.   Manufacturers Hanover

23.   Eastman Kodak

24.   Xerox

25. Proctor & Gamble

26. Goodyear

27. Phillips Petroleum

28. F. W. Woolworth

29. Union Carbide

30. Colgate-Palmolive

31. United Technologies

32. Dart & Kraft

33. Tenneco

34. CPC International

35. Chemical New York

36. Pan Am World Airways

37. R. J. Reynolds Industries

38. Coca-Cola

39. Bankers Trust New York

40. Minnesota Mining & Manufacturing

41. Continental Illinois

42. Johnson & Johnson

43. Atlantic Richfield

44. Getty Oil

45. Chrysler

46. International Harvester

47. Sperry

48. Halliburton

49. First Chicago

Table 2 (contd.)

50. Beatrice Foods

51. Monsanto

52. General Foods

53. General Telephone & Electronics

54. Sears, Roebuck

55. Nabisco Brands

56. American Express

57. Fluor

58. Trans World Airlines

59. Pfizer

60. Union Oil of California

61. American Brands

62. NCR

63. Hewlett-Packard

64. Caterpillar Tractor

65. First National Bank of Boston

66. PepsiCo

67. Allied Corporation

68. Honeywell

69. American International Group

70. Deere

71. Firestone

72. K mart

73. Continental Group

74. Warner-Lambert

75. Consolidated Foods

76. H. J. Heinz

77. RCA

78. W. R. Grace

79. American Home Products

80. Gulf & Western Industries

81. Burroughs

82. Merck

83. Irving Bank

84. Texas Instruments

85. Gillette

86. Scott Paper

87. Bendix

88. American Cyanamid

89. TRW

90. Bristol-Myers

91. Ralston Purina

92. Digital Equipment

93. Avon Products

94. Westinghouse Electric

95. Motorola

96. Litton Industries

Table 2 (contd.)

---

97. Marine Midland Banks

98. Philip Morris

99. Singer

100. Ingersoll-Rand

Results of Survey

The findings discussed below represent summaries of the detailed survey exhibits furnished in the appendix.

Statement Used

For their 1981 financial statements, the companies were allowed to select the method of foreign currency translation that they preferred — the method required by *Statement No. 8* or the method required by *Statement No. 52*. The survey showed that seventy-five percent of the sample companies followed *Statement No. 8*, while twenty-five percent followed *Statement No. 52*. In those cases where there was no mention of foreign currency translation, it was assumed that *Statement No. 8* was used since there was no indication of an accounting change to *Statement No. 52* in those instances. Ten percent of the companies did not mention their foreign currency translation methods. However, their disclosures indicated that *Statement No. 8* was used.

Adoption of the new statement did not always remove the need for the temporal method of translation. Of the sample companies using the new statement, sixty-eight percent specifically noted the use of both the current rate and temporal methods of translation in order to comply with the requirements of the new statement. Also, only 25 percent of the sample companies opted for early adoption and, in every case, the change resulted in an increase in earnings for the company.

Reporting Practices

Statement No. 8 and 52 each call for certain minimum reporting requirements. All of the companies were found to comply with these minimum requirements when the question of materiality was taken into consideration. That is, even though some companies did not provide the called-for minimum disclosures, those items which were not disclosed were deemed to be immaterial by the companies and their auditors. As a result, 23 percent of the companies still using the old statement did not even disclose the amount of the translation gain or loss, but they are still considered to be in compliance with the guidelines of the statement. Thirty-five percent of these companies specifically said the amount was insignificant. Another 35 percent of these companies lumped the amount of the translation gain or loss together with other items so that it was not distinguishable. The other 30 percent of these companies merely ignored the translation gain or loss. In addition, 8 percent of the sample companies using the new statement did not present an analysis of the cumulative translation adjustment.

Although some companies disclosed more information than others in this area, there were no cases of truly outstanding reporting. In most instances, the companies supplied the minimum information required and nothing more. Nineteen percent of the sample companies still using the old statement did report the effects of translating some of the cost of goods sold components, such as inventory and depreciation, at the historic exchange rates rather than at the average current exchange rates used to translate sales. Of these companies, 64 percent gave the specific amount of the effect while the other 36 percent only gave the directional impact on gross margin or earnings. Surprisingly, only 6 percent of all the sample companies identified the foreign currencies having a major impact upon foreign currency translations.

There was also a fair amount of diversity in the manner in which the information relating to foreign currency translation was displayed. Thirteen percent of the sample companies disclosed their "exchange gain or loss" as a line item on the income statement. Fifty percent of the companies disclosed foreign currency translation information in the footnotes to the financial statements. Forty-eight percent of the companies discussed foreign currency translation information in the management discussion and analysis sections of their annual reports. Twenty-two percent of the companies disclosed their cumulative foreign currency translation adjustments on the balance sheets as a separate component of stockholders' equity. Thirteen percent of the companies presented an analysis of their cumulative foreign currency translation adjustments as parts of the statement of change in stockholders' equity and 10 percent of the companies presented the analyses in the footnotes to the financial statements.

Disclosure Illustrations

In order to further clarify the nature of reporting practices in the area of foreign currency translation, this section will provide some specific examples of reporting by various companies. These examples will be subjectively grouped into three categories: below average disclosure, average disclosure, or above average disclosure.

Below Average Disclosure

One of the prime examples of below average disclosure was attributed to the General Motors Corporation. Despite the fact that foreign currency exchange and translation gains amounted to roughly 68 percent of net income for the year, General Motors limited its disclosure to the following footnote:

Foreign Exchange

Exchange and translation activity included in net income amounted to gains of $226.2 million in 1981, $164.6 million in 1980 and $86.2 million in 1979. Statement of Financial Accounting Standards (SFAS) No. 8, Accounting for the Translation of Foreign Currency Transactions and Foreign Currency Financial Statements, was applied throughout the three-year period.[1]

In light of the fact that foreign currency exchange and translation gains comprised a significant portion of net income, this limited disclosure was deemed inadequate. However, it did meet the minimum requirements of *Statement No. 8*, even though statement users were given no idea of what portions represented exchange (realized) gains and translation (unrealized) gains.

A second example of below average disclosure in the area of foreign currency translation is that of Honeywell Incorporated.[2] In this instance, foreign currency "exchange" gains amounted to approximately 32 percent of net income for 1981. However, Honeywell's disclosure was limited to the following footnote:

Foreign Currency Exchange Gains (Losses)

	1981	1980	1979
Honeywell and Subsidiaries	$16.8	$10.3	$(6.9)
Equity Companies	65.2	7.2	(2.1)
	$82.0	$17.5	$(9.0)

(Source: Honeywell Incorporated, Annual Report, 1981, p. 33).

As in the case of General Motors, Honeywell met the minimum disclosure requirements of FASB *Statement No. 8,* although the nature of the "exchange gains" was undefined. Unfortunately, on an item of this significance the minimum disclosure requirements of this statement do not provide sufficient information for the financial statement user to make an adequate assessment of the company's performance or situation.

A third example of below average disclosure of foreign currency matters is that of RCA, which elected early application of FASB *Statement No. 52.* In keeping with the requirements of the new statement, RCA disclosed a cumulative foreign currency translation adjustment of $(25,000,000) as a reduction of the stockholders' equity section of the December 31, 1981 balance sheet. Additional disclosure was provided in the footnotes.

Included in the Summary of Accounting Policies was a section on foreign currency translation noting the change in accounting policy and its effect.

Effective January 1, 1981, RCA adopted the Financial Accounting Standards Board Statement No. 52, "Foreign Currency Translation" (FAS No. 52). The effect on net income of applying this new Statement for the year ended December 31, 1981, was to add $9.1 million, or 12 cents per share. Prior years have not been restated.[3]

This amounts to an increase of twenty percent when calculated on the basis of the change in net income, but an increase of thirty-nine percent when calculated on the basis of the change in earnings per share.

In the later footnote on foreign currency translation, RCA disclosed the amount of foreign currency "exchange" losses included in income and the changes in the cumulative foreign currency translation adjustment for the year.

Foreign currency exchange losses computed in accordance with FAS No. 52 and included in net income for the year ended December 31, 1981, were $5 million. Foreign currency exchange losses computed in accordance with FAS No. 8 amounted to $1 million and $4 million for the years ended December 31, 1980 and 1979, respectively.

The amount established as a translation charge on January 1, 1981, after applying FAS No. 52 was $6.7 million. The aggregate amount of translation charges for the year ended December 31, 1981, was $18.3 million, which is net of $3.1 million transferred to net income as a result of the sale of foreign investments.4

Foreign currency "exchange" losses included in net income amounted to nine percent of net income. This is in addition to the effects of the change in accounting policy on net income. Also, the cumulative foreign currency translation adjustment practically tripled during 1981. In spite of these effects, RCA provided only minimum disclosure in the area of foreign currency translation. For example, although it did disclose both the cumulative foreign currency translation adjustment as a separate section of stockholders' equity in the balance sheet and the foreign currency "exchange" losses included in income, it did not discuss the fact that both the current rate and the temporal methods of translation were used. It also failed to discuss the reasons for using both methods. Was it because in certain cases the reporting currency was also the functional currency, or was it because the foreign functional currency experienced a high degree of inflation as defined by *Statement No. 52*? By neglecting to address such important questions, RCA limited the usefulness of its disclosures in this area.

Average Disclosure

One example of average disclosure of foreign currency effects was found in the annual report of Mobil Corporation. As part of the management review discussion on Foreign Refining and Marketing earnings, Mobil noted that

The benefit of a $120 million reversal of prior years' deferred tax provisions related to inventories in the United Kingdom was partially offset by unfavorable balance sheet foreign exchange translation losses of $59 million, an increase of $23 million from 1980.5

However, the main body of its disclosure was presented in the footnotes to the financial statements.

As a result of translating foreign currency balance sheet items into United States dollars, on an FAS 8 basis, net foreign currency translation losses of $44 million in 1981, $29 million in 1980, and $50 million in 1979, were charged against income.6

While Mobil did not provide more in-depth disclosures than those companies classified as examples of below average disclosure, the impact of foreign currency translation on net income was much less significant. In the case of Mobil Corporation, net foreign currency translation losses amounted to slightly less than two percent of net income for the year ended December 31, 1981.

Another example of average disclosure was found in the annual report of American Express Company. The cumulative foreign currency translation adjustment of $(6) million was shown separately as a reduction of the stockholders' equity section of the balance sheet. The analysis of changes in the cumulative foreign currency translation adjustment was shown as part of the consolidated statement of common shareholders' equity. Due to the way in which the statement was applied, there was no beginning balance in the adjustment account. Therefore, the change during the year and the ending balance were the same.

As part of a summary of significant accounting policies, American Express disclosed its method of accounting for foreign currency translation.

> Effective January 1, 1981 the Company adopted the newly issued Statement No. 52 of the Financial Accounting Standards Board, "Foreign Currency Translation." Foreign currency assets and liabilities are translated into their U.S. dollar equivalents based on rates of exchange generally prevailing at the end of the year. Revenue and expense accounts are generally translated at exchange rates prevailing during the year. Aggregate exchange gains and losses arising from the translation of foreign assets and liabilities and from certain foreign currency transactions are included in Common Shareholders' Equity. (See Note 11 to the Consolidated Financial Statements.) Prior to 1981, major foreign currency fixed assets were translated at historical rates and gains and losses from the translation of foreign currency assets and liabilities were reflected in net income.[7]

Additional information concerning the effects of foreign currency translation on the net income of American Express Company was disclosed elsewhere in the footnotes to the financial statements.

> Foreign currency transaction gains in 1981 amounted to $28 million, net of tax. The effect on net income from the translation of foreign currency assets and liabilities and from foreign currency transactions amounted to net gains of $21 million and $18 million in 1980 and 1979, respectively. These amounts for 1980 and 1979 have not been restated to reflect the change in accounting for foreign currency translation and certain foreign currency transactions resulting from the adoption of Statement No. 52 of the Financial Accounting Standards Board. The effect on 1981 net income of adopting Statement No. 52 is not material.[8]

As in the case of Mobil Corporation, American Express Company did not present more in-depth disclosures than those companies classified as examples of below average disclosure. However, once again the relative impacts of foreign currency translation on the reported financial information of American Express was not as significant as with the companies presenting below average disclosures.

Above Average Disclosure

An example of above average disclosure was found in the annual report of International Business Machines Corporation (IBM). In management's discussion of the results of operations, IBM noted the following facts concerning foreign currency translation.

1. The increase in gross income from non-United States operations for 1981 of only 1.4 percent resulted principally from the effects of the strengthening United States dollar.

2. The translation effect of a stronger United States dollar held down rental income growth.

3. "The rapid fall of major foreign currencies against the U.S. dollar in late 1980 and in 1981 was unprecedented in recent times (graphs illustrating these relationships appear on page 31 [of the report]). While a strong dollar may benefit the United States economy in many ways, the abruptness and magnitude of these currency changes had an adverse effect on IBM's consolidated financial results. Had currency rates remained constant year-to-year, and if the effects of currency rate changes on business volumes, pricing and other operating decisions were disregarded, it is estimated that consolidated gross income for 1981 would have been over $2 billion greater, and net earnings over $600 million greater."[9]

4. The strong surge in United States currency significantly affected period-to-period gross profit margin comparisons. "For example, non-U.S. gross income from rentals was adversely affected by the current exchange rates, but with no favorable impact on depreciation costs which are translated at historical exchange rates."[10]

5. "The strengthened U.S. dollar had a beneficial effect on selling, development, engineering and general and administrative expense by reducing the non-U.S. component of these expenses when translated into dollars."[11]

6. "The company recorded exchange gains in 1981 of $94 million. These gains resulted primarily from the translation of assets and liabilities recorded or denominated in currencies other than the U.S. dollar. This compares with an exchange gain of $24 million for 1980. Such gains are principally unrealized."[12]

7. The variance in the consolidated effective income tax rate from 1980 to 1981 reflect higher effective tax rates on non-United States

earnings which resulted primarily from the impact of currency translation.

8. "Sharp changes in foreign currency rates may again have short-term effects. But the increasing demand for IBM products and services, and the productivity they deliver, should assure a long-range trend of steady and sustained real growth in business volumes and financial performances."[13]

In addition to reviewing the results of operations, the management discussion section of IBM's annual report also commented on the financial condition of the company. That section of the report detailed the following information.

1. IBM "negotiated currency swap agreements with the World Bank, which effectively eliminated the foreign exchange risk associated with the $254 million German mark and $112 million Swiss franc loans undertaken in 1980."[14]

2. "Despite periodic shortages of capital, high interest rates, and dramatic shifts in currency exchange rates, IBM has been able to utilize its high credit rating and acquire appropriate levels of financing through worldwide sources. IBM has frequently borrowed in currencies other than the U.S. dollar. While there are risks associated with foreign currency obligations, there are also clear advantages. Interest rates are often much lower than comparable dollar loans, and the exchange loss risk associated with repayment is minimized by the availability of foreign source income in most major countries. Consequently, the company has considerable financing flexibility in many different currencies throughout the world."[15]

3. The ability to assess the funding requirements resulting from large capital investments exerting pressure on operational cash flow is complicated by uncertain economic conditions, particularly inflation, volatile interest rates, and foreign currency fluctuations.[16]

The footnotes to IBM's financial statements also included foreign currency translation information. The method of accounting for foreign currency translation was discussed along with other significant accounting policies.

Assets and liabilities denominated in currencies other than U.S. dollars are translated to U.S. dollars at year-end exchange rates, except that inventories and plant, rental machines and other property are translated at approximate rates prevailing when acquired. Income and expense items are translated at average rates of exchange prevailing during the year, except that inventories charged to cost of sales and depreciation are translated at historical rates. Exchange gains and losses are included in earnings currently.[17]

In a footnote discussing its non-United States operations, IBM reiterated the negative impact of foreign currency exchange rate changes on the reported results. It noted that despite a

strong performance, non-United States financial results were affected even more than United States operations by inflation and other factors. Adding to these conditions was the severe impact of the stronger United States dollar. The Management Discussion on page 23 [of the report] referred to this effect in greater detail. The graphs on the following page further illustrate the decline in value, in relation to the dollar, of the five major foreign currencies in which IBM conducts most of its non-United States business.[18]

Also included in the footnotes, were graphs of the changes in relation to the dollar of the five major foreign currencies in which IBM conducted operations. These graphs were shown independently of any discussion regarding specific changes (see fig. 5).

Disclosures in the annual report of Avon Products, Inc. were also judged to be above average. In the management discussion section of its report, Avon noted that "during 1981, Statement of Financial Accounting Standards No. 52 relating to foreign currency translation was adopted, and the results of 1980 have been restated to reflect this change."[19] Avon also noted the following items in its discussion:

1. "The strengthening of the U.S. dollar abroad and unsettled economic conditions in some of the Company's major foreign markets were significant factors contributing to the decline in International sales. Although sales in Europe increased in terms of local currencies, European sales after translation into U.S. dollars fell 17%. Avon sales in terms of U.S. dollars in Latin America advanced 6%, and in Canada, the Pacific and Africa combined 10%."[20]

2. "The increase in the cost ratio was primarily the result of competitive pricing strategies in the U.S. and abroad and the effect of foreign currency fluctuations."[21]

3. One of the factors contributing to the increase in the "interest income and other income" category was "greater foreign exchange gains, resulting from the remeasurement of foreign currency state-

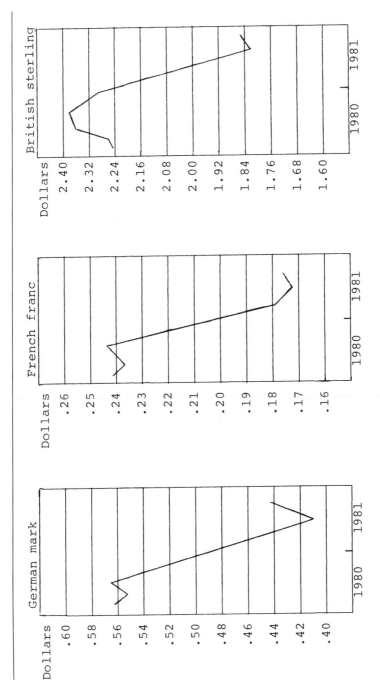

Figure 5. Foreign Currency Valued in U.S. Dollars

Figure 5 (contd.)

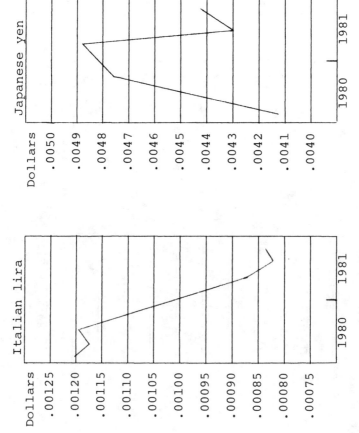

ments into U.S. dollars, and realized and unrealized foreign currency transactions in 1981, compared with 1980."[22]

4. "The greater foreign exchange gains included in other income in 1981 were more than offset by higher foreign exchange losses charged to cost of goods sold and to expenses, which resulted from the remeasurement of inventories and prepaid expenses at historical rates. The net effect of these factors reduced net earnings by $36.7 million (61¢ per share) in 1981, compared with $20.0 million (33¢ per share) in 1980."[23]

5. "The principal cause of the increase in the effective tax rate was higher tax rates on International earnings resulting from foreign exchange losses."[24]

Foreign currency translation information was also shown in other sections of the financial statements. The cumulative foreign currency translation adjustment for 1981 of $(19.7) million was shown as a separate item reducing the stockholders' equity section of the balance sheet. The effect of foreign currency translation adjustments on working capital of $2.6 million was shown along with the uses of working capital in the statement of changes in financial position. Other effects of foreign currency translation were discussed in the footnotes to the financial statements. Included in a schedule of differences between the consolidated income tax rate and the statutory federal income tax rate, was the effect of remeasuring foreign currency statements, which increased the consolidated income tax rate by 3.3 percent. Elsewhere in the footnotes the effects of foreign exchange fluctuations were disclosed as shown in figure 6.[25]

The examples of reporting presented in this section have been selected and classified subjectively. Furthermore, classification was made on a comparative rather than an absolute basis. Therefore, those examples classified as above average are not intended to be examples of excellent disclosure practices; even the above average examples are flawed. However, they do illustrate management efforts toward improved disclosures.

Conclusion

The results of this survey support the criticism of Shank and Shamis,[26] Norby,[27] and others who have expressed concern over the inadequacies of the disclosure requirements governing foreign currency translation. In varying forms, these authors have called for improvements, including fuller disclosure and a separate, somewhat more standardized presentation format for reporting the effects of foreign currency translation on the organi-

Figure 6. Effect of Foreign Exchange Fluctuations

Net earnings were unfavorably affected by foreign exchange fluctuations, as follows (in millions):

	Year Ended December 31,		
	1981	1980	1979
Foreign exchange gains (losses)-net:			
Remeasurement of foreign currency statements into U.S. dollars, and realized and unrealized foreign currency transactions..............	$ 10.2	$ .3	$ 4.2
Remeasurement of certain items, principally inventories, at historical rates..	(46.9)	(20.3)	(23.3)
	$(36.7)	$(20.0)	$(19.1)
Detail by country:			
Brazil...............	$(19.6)	$(15.8)	$(15.6)
Argentina...........	(15.6)	(2.9)	(4.5)
All other-net........	(1.5)	(1.3)	1.0)
	$(36.7)	$(20.0)	$(19.1)

An analysis of adjustment-foreign currency translation (in the shareholders' equity section of the statement of financial condition) for the three years ended December 31, 1981 follows (in millions):

	1981	1980	1979
Adjustment-foreign currency translation:			
Balance, January 1	$ 15.2	$ 18.0	$ 11.6
Translation adjustments..............	(34.9)	(2.8)	6.4
Balance, December 31	$(19.7)	$ 15.2	$ 18.0

(Source: Avon Products, Incorporated, 1981 Annual Report, p. 46).

zation. Using these ideas as a basic foundation in the following chapter, a more informative disclosure model will be constructed. The model suggested will attempt to provide the financial statement user with a more intelligible presentation of the pertinent information, thus enabling more meaningful analyses and evaluations.

6

Proposed Disclosure Model

Introduction

The objective of this chapter will be to develop a more informative disclosure model. This model will be aimed at improving the availability and presentation of foreign currency translation information so that the financial statement user will be able to draw more meaningful conclusions from the information being presented. The suggested improvements will employ supplementary disclosures using a matrix presentation format along with management explanations and discussions.

Presentation Format

The combination of matrix presentation and management discussion provides for an efficient method of disclosing a significant amount of useful information. This is particularly important in a highly controversial area such as foreign currency translation, since it allows the statement users to make the adjustments that they deem necessary for their purposes.

The Matrices

The use of three separate matrices is suggested. The first matrix would disclose the balance sheet effects of translation along with the foreign currency transaction gains and losses (see fig. 7). This matrix is based on the one suggested by Shank and Shamis.[1] The rows represent the major currencies involved and the columns represent the various components of the exchange gain or loss. These components include:

1. Realized transaction gains and losses
   Example: The difference between the translated amount of an account payable on the transaction date and on the settlement date.

Figure 7. Balance Sheet Effects Matrix

Currency	Translation Method Used	Transaction Gains and Losses		Translation Gains and Losses			
				Realized	Unrealized		
		Realized	Unrealized		Likely to be Realized		Unlikely to be Realized
					Short Term	Long Term	
Total							
		A	B	C	E		F

Column
A = Realized conversion gains and losses on closed foreign currency transactions.
B = Unrealized exchange gains and losses on open foreign currency transactions.
C = Realized exchange gains and losses resulting from the translation of foreign financial statements.
D = Unrealized exchange gains and losses resulting from the translation of foreign financial statements which are likely to be realized in the short term.
E = Unrealized exchange gains and losses resulting from the translation of foreign financial statements which are likely to be realized in the long term.
F = Unrealized exchange gains and losses resulting from the translation of foreign financial statements which are unlikely to be realized.

2. Unrealized transaction gains and losses
   Example: The difference between the translated amount of an
   account payable on the transaction date and the intervening balance sheet date.

3. Realized translation gains and losses
   Example: The portion of the cumulative translation adjustment
   transferred to income when the related foreign investment was liquidated.

4. Unrealized translation gains and losses likely to be realized in the
   short run
   Example: Where the foreign operation was a sales outlet for the
   parent (selling products and remitting the proceeds to
   the parent upon collection), the portion of the translation gain or loss likely to be realized upon remittance
   would be an example of an unrealized translation gain
   or loss likely to be realized in the short run.

5. Unrealized translation gains and losses likely to be realized in the
   long run
   Example: The foreign operation was in the developmental stages
   and cash flows were mainly from parent to subsidiary.
   In the future, once the subsidiary was established, the
   situation would reverse and the cash flows would be
   from subsidiary to parent. The portion of the translation gain or loss expected to be realized when the reversal takes place would be an example of an unrealized
   translation gain or loss likely to be realized in the long
   run.

6. Unrealized translation gains and losses unlikely to be realized
   Example: A foreign operation that was an autonomous unit and
   reinvested its earnings rather than making cash remittances to the parent would be an example of a situation
   in which translation gains and losses were unlikely to
   be realized.

In addition to the above components, there is also a column for disclosing
the method of translation used: (1) Current rate, and (2) Temporal. This
matrix will be referred to as the "Balance Sheet Effects Matrix," since
primary emphasis is placed upon disclosures of unrealized translation differences.

Not only would this matrix break the foreign exchange gain or loss down into its real and nominal (unreal or "paper") components, but it would further classify the nominal components in accordance with their likely disposition. Thus, the matrix could aid the statement user in weighing the relative importance of the various components presented. As the time frame prior to expected realization increased, the chance for a reversal of the gain or loss (or for other changes to take place) would also increase. This would compound the uncertainty of eventual realization.

In addition, breaking the various components of the translation differences down into the major currencies involved should highlight any portfolio effects responsible for reducing the net amount of the translation gain or loss. Based on the Markowitz-Tobin Mean Variance Model,[2] it can be shown that the variance from a portfolio of currencies is generally less than the sum of the variance of each currency in the portfolio. A firm might have a natural portfolio of currencies as a result of the nature of its cash flows and the distribution of its assets and liabilities across currencies. The amount of diversification obtained would depend on the covariance of exchange rate changes. Changes in the portfolio of currencies or their interrelationships could have important implications. For example, assume that Company A had a translation loss of $30,000 as a result of its investment in German marks and a translation gain of $30,000 as a result of its investment in Japanese yen. As a result, the translation gain and loss netted to zero. If these currency trends continued and the investment in marks was liquidated, Company A could expect to experience translation losses in the future. Detailing the translation gains or losses according to their components and by the major currencies involved would allow the statement user to make a more intelligent assessment of the possible impact of related changes.

The second matrix would facilitate the presentation of the major income statement effects of foreign currency translation (see fig. 8). The importance of such disclosures has been noted by several authors, including Shank and Shamis[3] and Norby.[4] The rows would present the major currencies involved. The first column would indicate the translation method that was used: temporal or current rate. The remaining columns would be used to disclose the various income statement effects of foreign currency translation. These effects include:

1.   General effect — the translation gain or loss resulting from translating this year's income statement at a different rate than last year's income statement.

2.   Cost of goods sold effect — the realized exchange gain or loss included in cost of goods sold which resulted from translating

Figure 8. Income Statement Effects Matrix

Currency	Translation Method Used	General	Cost of Goods Sold	Interest Expense	Income Tax	Investment Income	Other
Total							
		A	B	C	D	E	F

Column

A = Translation gain or loss resulting from translating the current year's income statement at a different rate than last year's income statement

B = Realized exchange gain or loss included in cost of goods sold resulting from the translation of inventory and depreciation at historical exchange rates while translating sales at the average current rate

C = The dollar equivalent change in interest expense on foreign debt resulting from changes in the exchange rate when interest expense is translated at the average current rate

D = Tax impact of foreign currency adjustments

E = Portion of investment income that results from foreign currency adjustment rather than from the operations of the 20%-50% owned affiliates accounted for on an equity basis

F = Other important income statement effects not yet disclosed inventory and depreciation at historical exchange rates under the temporal method of translation while other income statement items, such as sales, were translated at the average current exchange rate.

3. Interest expense effect—the dollar equivalent change in interest expense on foreign debt resulting from changes in the exchange rate when interest expense is translated at the average current exchange rate.

4. Income tax effects—the tax impact of items included in the overall exchange gain or loss (an alternative would be to show the items on both a before- and after-tax basis).

5. Investment income effects—the proportion of investment income that is attributable to foreign exchange gains and losses rather than to operations of the twenty-percent to fifty-percent owned affiliates accounted for on an equity basis.

6. Other—any other important income statement effects not yet disclosed (for example, contractual commitments denominated in the foreign currency).

The above disclosures were considered important for a number of reasons. First of all, they would highlight the fact that there were a number of items in the income statement affected by foreign currency translation. Without such disclosure, this fact could be obscured—giving the erroneous impression that only balance sheet items were affected. The disclosures also would make a more comprehensive analysis possible. Neglecting to disclose the income statement effects would be to ignore a possibly significant aspect of translation.

The disclosure of the general effect should help to clarify the change in income resulting solely from the change in the average current rate used to translate the income statement.

Disclosing the cost of goods sold effects should assist the statement user in identifying the resulting distortion on profit margins and net income. It would also allow the user to make any adjustments that he deemed necessary to his analysis.

The disclosure of interest expense, income tax, investment income, and other important effects of translation would further highlight the fact that the various income statement items were affected. It would be a move away from concentrating on the "bottom line" (net income) to the exclusion of other factors. Income tax effect disclosures could also help to clarify a confusing area. In some cases, the income tax effects can reverse the effect of translation. A before-tax gain can become an after-tax loss and vice versa.

With this broader disclosure, the statement users would be provided with the information necessary to direct their attention to the complexities of translation. No longer would the statement user be forced to settle for aggregate information that obscured important details.

A third matrix would disclose the effects of foreign currency translation on earnings per share (EPS) (see fig. 9). An example of such a matrix was given in *Fortune*[5] as part of a discussion on the effects of FASB *Statement No. 8*. As in the matrices in Figures 7 and 8, the rows would represent the major currencies involved and the first column would indicate the method of translation used. The remaining columns would furnish information on earnings per share and the relevant changes. This information will include:

1. Last year's earnings per share, as reported.

2. This year's earnings per share, as reported.

3. This year's earnings per share, assuming that the exchange rate did not change. This would allow a comparison of the current year's earnings per share and last year's earnings without the distorting effects of translation.

4. The total effect on earnings per share of exchange rate adjustments. This would highlight the effect of translation on earnings per share.

5. The portion of the effect on earnings per share resulting from exchange rate adjustments to balance sheet items. This would identify the effect that translating foreign balance sheets had on the consolidated earnings per share of the company.

6. The portion of the effect on earnings per share resulting from exchange rate adjustments to income statement items. This would identify the effect that translating foreign income statements had on the consolidated earnings per share of the company.

This matrix could be designated the "EPS Effects Matrix."

The information in this matrix would be useful to the financial statement user in his analysis of earnings per share. It would also be in keeping with the objectives of *Accounting Principles Board Opinion No. 15*, "Earnings per Share," which stated:

Figure 9.   Earnings per Share Effects Matrix

| Currency | Translation Method Used | Earnings Per Share | | | Effect on EPS of Exchange Rate Adjustments | | |
| | | Last Year | This Year | | | From Adjustments to | |
		As Reported	As Reported	Assuming Exchange Rates Did Not Change	Total	Balance Sheet Items	Income Statement Items
Total							
		A	B	C	D	E	F

Column

 A   = Reported earnings per share from the previous year
 B   = Reported earnings per share for the current year
 C   = Earnings per share that would have been reported for the current year if exchange rates had
        not changed
 D   = Total effect on earnings per share resulting from translation: D = B - C; D = E + F
 E   = Effect on earnings per share resulting from the translation of balance sheet items
 F   = Effect on earnings per share resulting from the translation of income statement items

> Earnings per share data are used in evaluating the past operating performance of a business in forming an opinion as to its potential and in making investment decisions.
> . . .
>
> In view of the widespread use of earnings per share data, it is important that such data be computed on a consistent basis and presented in the most meaningful manner.[6]

Therefore, where changes in earnings per share result solely from translation, that fact should be disclosed. The EPS Effects Matrix could accomplish this task.

While the matrices can do an excellent job of quantifying the impact of translation on the financial statements, there is still need for additional disclosure. Some items are very difficult, if not impossible, to quantify. For this reason, it is recommended that management discussion be used in conjunction with the matrices in order to provide as complete a picture as possible to the financial statement user.

Management Discussion

Here the function of management discussion would be twofold. First, it would clarify the information presented in the matrices where necessary. Secondly, it would provide additional information concerning foreign currency translation that was deemed useful to the financial statement user.

Clarifying the information already presented in the matrices would usually involve answering questions, such as what type of transactions or activities led to the effects, and is this trend likely to continue? For example, a portion of the transaction losses may have resulted from the purchase of merchandise from certain sources that are no longer used. Clarification would not be necessary in every case. However, where it could provide useful, significant information, it should be done.

Another aspect of management discussion involves the presentation of additional information. The type of information presented in this section will vary depending on the circumstances. In each instance, it would be necessary to determine what information has not yet been disclosed but would be useful for decision making purposes. Possible topics might well include:

1.   Management's response to the effects of translation and to changes in the exchange rate.

2.   Hedging activities
    a.   Engaged in
        1.   Type
        2.   Extent

      b. Planned
          1. Type
          2. Extent

3. Changes in sales prices
   a. Instituted
   b. Restrictions

4. Estimate of the effects of changes in the exchange rates on sales volume

5. Estimate of the effects of changes in the exchange rates on expense levels

6. Resulting economic effects of possible volume, price, and expense level changes

7. Special advantages or disadvantages of the foreign operating environments

8. Management's outlook for the future in this area.

In addition, the analysis of changes during the period in the separate component of equity for cumulative translation adjustments could be presented here along with an explanation of those changes. Other types of information considered to be useful could also be presented here.

Conclusion

Together, the matrix information and management discussion would provide a solid base for decision making purposes. While all aspects of this model would not apply to every situation, it would simply be necessary to apply those aspects of the model which were relevant to that particular company. Thus, the model is not designed to be a rigid framework for reporting, but, rather, it would serve as a *flexible* reporting framework as an aid to be used in disclosing all relevant information in the area.

    In essence, the model would: (1) provide a more definitive approach to the disclosure of the effects of foreign currency translation; (2) present information that would enable a more critical financial analysis of the positive and negative aspects of the major international markets being served; and (3) be flexible enough to accommodate a wide variety of situations and changing circumstances.

    In addition, significant advantages could well accrue (and surely would) to prudent managements who recognize that the benefits of management discussions facilitate an understanding of the company's past performance and future possibilities.

7

Conclusion

The area of foreign currency translation is extremely complex. As such, it would be unrealistic to assume that acceptable solutions to the problems delineated will be simple or forthcoming in the near future. Therefore, it would be remiss not to at least touch upon two somewhat unusual approaches that could be adopted in the future. Then, the disclosure model suggested in this paper will be evaluated as a practicable, interim solution using the latest criteria for reporting concepts.

Futuristic Proposals

Two futuristic proposals will be examined in this section. They are (1) the use of purchasing power ratios, and (2) discontinuing the consolidation of foreign financial statements.

Purchasing Power Parity Ratios

As noted earlier, the use of exchange rates in foreign currency translation is a complicating factor. One suggestion for removing this complication is the use of purchasing-power-parity ratios in place of exchange rates in the translation process. The use of such ratios — developed to reflect the relative purchasing powers of the respective currencies in their domestic environments at a given time — would make more economic sense than the use of exchange rates, which are subject to the vagaries of the foreign exchange markets and do not necessarily represent the relative purchasing powers of the currencies involved.

Currently, such purchasing power parity ratios do not exist on a large scale. However, they could be developed using appropriately weighted market baskets of goods and services for the industry and environment.[1] Given ready availability — which is doubtful, at best — many of the disclosure problems addressed in this paper would persist.

Discontinuing the Consolidation of Foreign Financial Statements

The intended purpose of consolidated financial statements is to clarify information for the financial statement user by reporting the results of a consolidated group of companies as though they were the results of a single entity. Unfortunately, when foreign financial statements are involved, consolidation often conceals more information than it reveals.

As a solution to this problem and in the interest of informative disclosure, it has been suggested that the consolidation of foreign financial statements be discontinued.[2] Instead of consolidating the results of foreign operations, these results could be shown separately and in comparison with host country industrial averages. Other relevant information, such as cash available for dividends, dividends paid, and the translation factors used (such as the average exchange rates or purchasing-power ratios for the year, and the year-end exchange rates or purchasing-power ratios), should be shown along with descriptive disclosures. These descriptive disclosures would include a general statement of foreign accounting policies, pointing out the differences from United States generally accepted accounting principles. In addition, there would be a statement about foreign operations, including remarks about the political, legal, and social environments in each country.[3]

Given the entrenchment of consolidated statements as the *primary* financial reports in the United States, acceptance of the above suggestion — regardless of its merits — is considered unlikely at the present time. Eventual acceptance would probably depend upon the coming of age of present embryonic efforts toward segmented reportings under *FASB 14.*

During the Interim

The reporting model developed in the preceding chapter could prove useful as an interim measure. One of its chief advantages would be the flexibility it provides. Such a model would be able to meet the latest financial reporting criteria set forth in FASB *SFA Concepts No. 1*, "Objectives of Financial Reporting by Business Enterprises."

Reporting Criteria

The major reporting criteria established in *SFA Concepts No. 1* are as follows:

1. Financial reporting should provide information that is useful to potential investors and creditors and other users in making rational investments, credit, and similar decisions.[4]

2. Financial reporting should provide information to help present and potential investors and creditors and other users in assessing the amounts, timing, and uncertainty of prospective cash receipts from dividends or interest and the proceeds from the sale, redemption or maturity of securities or loans.[5]

3. Financial reporting should provide information about the economic resources of an enterprise, the claims to those resources (obligations of the enterprise to transfer resources to other entities and owners' equity), and the effects of transactions, events, and circumstances that change resources and claims to those resources.[6]

4. The primary focus of financial reporting is information about an enterprise's performance provided by measures of earnings and its components.[7]

5. Investors, creditors, and others often use reporting earnings and information about the components of earnings in various ways and for various purposes in assessing their prospects for cash flows from investments in or loans to an enterprise.[8]

6. Financial reporting should provide information about how management of an enterprise has discharged its stewardship responsibility to owners (stockholders) for the use of enterprise resources entrusted to it.[9]

7. Financial reporting should include explanations and interpretations to help users understand financial information provided.[10]

The Model

The disclosure model and management discussion presented in the preceding chapter satisfy the above criteria and can be implemented today.

By breaking down the "exchange gain or loss" into its real and nominal (paper) components, the model facilitates an analysis of the entity, the components of the entity's earnings, and the cash flow prospects. The model will also provide additional information about the nature of a firm's resources, the changes in the resources, and how management has discharged its stewardship responsibility. The management discussion section of the proposed model would be helpful in integrating these areas, and in providing the explanations and interpretations necessary to educate users and increase user understanding of the information provided. Naturally, refinements could (and would) be made to the proposed model as experience was gained by statement issuers and accountants.

Here it is important to recognize that raw data and normative methods are no longer appropriate for complex situations. Instead, explanations provided by managements and attestations by accountants are needed. In order to accomplish this:

1. More managements must recognize (or be convinced) that their credibility is largely a function of their candor. Inadequate disclosures are often perceived as equivalent to "taking the Fifth Amendment." On the other hand, "telling it like it is" implies not only an adequate disclosure of negative events but, also, improving the credibility of positive events and management's actions.

2.ʼ Accountants, on the other hand, must realize that the ability (and willingness) to interpret has differentiated them from bookkeepers (in the past) and computers (today). Shedding this reluctance to interpret and exercise judgment seems necessary if the profession wishes to come of age. Accountants also attest to the "fairness" of presentations. This implies the existence of criteria upon which they based their judgments.

3. Accounting standard setters must resist politicization and the tendency to seek and apply simplex solutions to complex issues. Instead, they must realize that the complexities of the business environments call for situational approaches—if reports are to make economic sense. FASB *Statement No. 52* is evidence, albeit minor, of a step in this direction. Reporting and disclosure requirements should be related with situations. Managements and accountants should be charged with exercising the judgments necessary in each situation.

Last, but certainly not least, the SEC will have a role to play. It might be passive or active, dependent upon the actions taken by the three aforementioned participants. In *Financial Reporting Release 6*, the SEC noted its concern about the adequacy of financial statement disclosure concerning the effects of translating foreign operations. The Commission encouraged publicly held companies to experiment with the form and content of disclosures on foreign operations and the effects of foreign currency translation under *Statement No. 52*. The Release also encouraged experimentation with narrative information on these topics—suggesting that management discussion and analysis should provide more information to supplement that provided in the financial statements.

This additional support could well provide the impetus necessary for managements to overcome their reluctance to provide information beyond the minimum requirements specified, thereby providing the statement user with a more useful set of financial statements. This would allow for a more critical financial analysis relating to the positive and negative aspects of the major international markets involved, while maintaining sufficient flexibility to fit a wide variety of situations and changing circumstances.

The flexibility of this model would also allow for changes in reporting befitting changes in circumstances without requiring the FASB to continually readdress the question in the form of official pronouncements. This would be a tremendous advantage today when the capabilities of the FASB are being strained by the proliferation of accounting statements. The FASB's tendency to follow a policy of "crisis management" in addressing accounting problems could have important implications. One of the major criticisms of the APB, eventually resulting in its demise, was its brush fire approach to accounting problems.

If the FASB does not adopt a more farsighted and flexible approach, it could suffer the same fate. Most likely the SEC would, reluctantly, exercise its authority to prescribe accounting and reporting standards. The accounting profession would be the lesser for it.

Appendix

Summary of Survey Data

The table presented in this appendix provides a summary of the data gathered in the survey of annual reports. Due to space limitations, the column headings will be numbered according to the following key.

Column 1. Company Stock Ticker Symbol

Column 2. Industry Code

Column 3. Statement used — No. 8 or No. 52

Column 4. Minimum disclosures
      A. Provided
      B. Not provided, but information considered insignificant
      C. Obscured

Column 5. Identified foreign currencies having a major impact on foreign currency translation

Column 6. "Exchange" gain or loss disclosed
      A. Separately
      B. As part of another item so that it was not distinguishable

Column 7. Effect of translating some cost of goods sold components at historic rates rather than the average current rates used to translate Sales
      A. Specific quantitative effect
          1. Inventory
          2. Depreciation
          3. Other
      B. Directional impact on gross margin or earnings
          1. Inventory
          2. Depreciation
          3. Other

Column 8. Method of translation used under 52
    A. Current Rate
    B. Temporal

Column 9. Cumulative translation adjustment

Column 10. Analysis of the cumulative translation adjustment
    A. Full analysis
    B. Only selected components allowing the statement user to prepare an analysis

Column 11. Body of financial statements
    A. Exchange gain or loss as line item on income statement
    B. Cumulative translation adjustment as a separate section of stockholders' equity
    C. Analysis of the cumulative translation adjustment
    D. Other

Column 12. Footnotes
    A. Exchange gain or loss
    B. Cumulative translation adjustment
    C. Analysis of cumulative translation adjustment
    D. Other

Column 13. Management discussion and analysis
    A. Exchange gain or loss
    B. Cumulative translation adjustment
    C. Analysis of cumulative translation adjustment
    D. Other

In the first column of the table, the companies were designated by their stock ticker symbols given below:

Scott Paper   SPP
Halliburton Company   HAL
Occidental Petroleum   OXY
Exxon Corporation   XON
Mobil Corporation   MOB
Texaco, Incorporated   TX
Standard Oil of California   SD
Phibro Solomon   PB
Gulf Oil   GO
Standard Oil of Indiana   SN
Sun Company   SUN
Phillips Petroleum   P

Atlantic Richfield   ARC
Getty Oil   GET
Union Oil of California   UCL
E.I. du Pont de Nemours   DD
Dow Chemical   DOW
Union Carbide   UK
Monsanto   MTC
Allied Corporation   ALD
W.R. Grace   GRA
American Cyanamid   ACY
General Electric   GE
Westinghouse Electric   WX
Texas Instruments   TXN
Deere & Company   DE
Caterpillar Tractor   CAT
International Harvester   HR
Ingersoll Rand   IR
Fluor Corporation   FLR
United Technologies   UTX
IBM   IBM
Sperry Corporation   SY
Honeywell, Incorporated   HON
Burroughs Corporation   BGH
TRW Incorporated   TRW
Digital Equipment   DEC
NCR Corporation   NCR
Xerox Corporation   XRX
Hewlett Packard   HWP
Continental Group Inc.   CCC
Ford Motor   F
General Motors   GM
Chrysler Corporation   C
Bendix   BX
Goodyear Tire   GT
Firestone   FIR
Singer Company   SMF
Motorola, Incorporated   MOT
Eastman Kodak   EK
Consolidated Foods   CFD
H.J. Heinz   HNZ
Proctor & Gamble   PG
Colgate Palmolive   CL

CPC International, Inc.   CPC
General Foods   GF
Ralston Purina   RAL
Nabisco Brands, Incorporated   NB
Dart & Kraft, Incorporated   DK
Beatrice Foods   BRY
Coca Cola   KO
Pepsi Company   PEP
Gillette   GS
Avon Products   AVP
R.J. Reynolds   RJR
American Brands   AMB
Philip Morris   MO
Pfizer Incorporated   PFE
Warner Lambert   WLA
American Home Products   AHP
Merck & Company   MRK
Bristol-Myers   BMY
Safeway Stores   SA
Sears Roebuck   S
F.W. Woolworth   Z
K Mart Corporation   KM
Johnson & Johnson   JNJ
GTE   GTE
Pan Am World Airways   PN
Trans World Corporation   TW
First Natl. Bank of Boston   FB
Citicorp   FNC
Chase Manhattan Corp.   CMB
J.P. Morgan & Company   JPM
Manufacturers Hanover   MHC
Chemical New York   CHL
Bankers Trust New York   BT
Irving Bank Corporation   V
Marine Midland Bank   MM
Continental Illinois Corp.   CIL
First Chicago Corporation   FNB
Bank America Corporation   BAC
American Express   AXP
American Intl. Group   AIGR
ITT   ITT
Tenneco, Incorporated   TGT

Minn. Mining & Mfg.   MMM
RCA Corporation   RCA
Gulf West Industries   GW
Litton Industries   LIT

The companies were arranged by industries — using the industry classifications and codes from *Industry Scope* given below:

Industry Codes	Industry Classification
001–082	Natural Resources
100–192	Industrial Products
200–248	Consumer Durables
300–391	Non-Durables
400–438	Retail Trade
500–562	Services
600–628	Utilities
700–724	Transportation
800–873	Finance
900	Multi-Industry

Table 3. Summary of Annual Report Survey

1	2	3	4	5	6	7	8	9	10	11	12	13
						Natural Resources						
SPP	031	52	A				A,B	X	B	B	A,B	
HAL	050	8	A		A						D		A
OXY	060	52	A		A		A,B	X	A	A,C	A	D
XON	070	8	A		A					A	A	
MOB	070	8	A		A						A	
TX	070	8	A	X	A						A	A,D
SD	070	8	A		A						D	A
PB	070	8	B								D	
GO	070	8	A		A						D	A
SN	070	8	A		A						A	

1	2	3	4	5	6	7	8	9	10	11	12	13
SUN	070	8	A	A	A						A	
P	070	8	A	A	A						A	A
ARC	070	8	A	X	A						A	
GET	070	8	A		A						A	
UCL	070	8	B									
DD	080	8	B								D	D
DOW	080	3	A		A					A	D	
UK	080	8	A	X	A	B					A	D
MTC	080	8	A		A	B					A	D
ALD	080	8	A		A				B		D	A,D
GRA	080	8	A		A	A		X		A	A	A
ACY	080	52	A		A	A-1	A,B	X	B	B	B,C	A

Table 3 (contd.)

Industrial Products

1	2	3	4	5	6	7	8	9	10	11	12	13
GE	100	8	A		A	B-1					A,D	
WX	100	8	B								D	D
TXN	112	8	B								D	
DE	120	8	A		A						A	D	A
CAT	121	8	A		A							A	D
HR	122	8	A		A	A						A	D
IR	125	52	A					A	X	B	B	C,D	
FLR	150	8	B									D	
UTX	160	52	A		A			A,B	X	A	B,C	A,D	A,D
IBM	170	8	A		A							D	A,D
SY	170	8	A		A						A		

1	2	3	4	5	6	7	8	9	10	11	12	13
HON	170	8	A		A						A	
BGH	170	8	B									D
TRW	170	52	A		A			X	A	B,C	A,D	
DEC	170	8	B								D	
NCR	171	8	A		A						A	D
XRX	172	52	A		A		A,B	X	A	B	A,C	
HWP	182	8	B								D	
CCC	190	52	A				A	X	A	B,C		D

Consumer Durables

1	2	3	4	5	6	7	8	9	10	11	12	13
F	200	8	A		A						A,D	
GM	200	8	A		A						A	

Table 3 (contd.)

1	2	3	4	5	6	7	8	9	10	11	12	13
C	200	8	B								D	
BX	201	8	A		A	B-1					A	
GT	210	52	A		A		A,B	X	A	A,B,C		D
FIR	210	8	A		A	A-1				A	A	D
SMF	230	8	A		A					A	D	D
MOT	231	8	A		A	A-1					A,D	D
EK	243	8	A		A						A	A
						Non Durables						
CFD	301	8	A		A							A
HNZ	301	8	A		A						D	A
PG	310	8	A		A	B-1					A	D

1	2	3	4	5	6	7	8	9	10	11	12	13
CL	310	52	A		A		A,B	X	A	B	A,C	D
CPC	311	8	A	X	A					A	D	A,D
GF	311	8	A		A						A,D	
RAL	311	8	A		A						A	
NB	312	8	A		A	A					A	
DK	322	52	A		A		A,B	X		B	A	
BRY	322	8	A		A	A-1					A	
KO	332	8	B							D	D	
PEP	332	8	A		A						A	D
GS	360	8	A		A						A	
AVP	360	52	A	X	A	B	A,B	X	A	A	A,C	D
RJR	380	8	A		A					A	D	

Table 3 (contd.)

1	2	3	4	5	6	7	8	9	10	11	12	13
AMB	380	52	C				A	X	B	B		D
MO	380	8	A		A	A-1					A,D	D
PFE	390	8	A		A						A	D
WLA	390	8	A		A	A					A	D
AHP	390	8	A		A						A	
MRK	390	8	A		A						A	D
BMY	390	8	A		A	A-1					A	D
					Retail Trade							
SA	400	8	A		A				A	A	D	A
S	410	52	A		A		A,B	X	A	B,C	A	A
Z	420	52	C				A	X	A	C		
KM	420	8	A		A		A				A	A

1	2	3	4	5	6	7	8	9	10	11	12	13
						Services						
JNJ	551	52	A		A		A,B	X	A	B	A,B	C
						Utilities						
GTE	600	52	C				A,B	X	A	B,C	D	
						Transportation						
PN	700	8			A						D	A
TW	700	8	A		A					A	D	D

Table 3 (contd.)

1	2	3	4	5	6	7	8	9	10	11	12	13
						Finance						
FB	800	8	C		B						A	
FNC	801	8	C	X	B							D
CMB	801	8	A		A						A	D
JPM	801	8	A		A						A	
MHC	801	8	C		B					D	D	
CHL	801	52	A		A		A,B	X	A	B,C	A,D	
BT	801	8	A									A
V	801	8	A		A						A,D	
MM	801	52	B		A		A,B	X	B	C	B	A
CIL	804	8	C	B	A		A,B				D	
FNB	804	52	A				A,B	X	A	B,C	A	

	1	2	3	4	5	6	7	8	9	10	11	12	13
BAC		809	52	A		A		A,B	X	B	B,C	A	D
AXP		810	52					A	X	B	B,C	D	
AIGR		830	8	A		A				A			
							Multi Industry						
ITT		900	52	A		A	A	A,B	X	A	B,C	A,D	B
TGT		900	8	A		A						A,D	
MMM		900	52	A				A	X	B	B,C	D	
RCA		900	52	A		A		A,C	X	B	B	A,C	
GW		900	8	C		B						D	
LIT		900	8	A		A					A	D	

Notes

Chapter 1

1. Financial Accounting Standards Board, *Statement of Financial Accounting Concepts No. 1*, "Objectives of Financial Reporting by Business Enterprises" (Stamford, Conn.: FASB, 1981), par. 34.

2. Ibid., par. 37.

3. Ibid., par. 40.

4. Ibid., par. 54.

Chapter 2

1. Jacob A. Frenkel and Harry G. Johnson (eds.), *The Economics of Exchange Rates: Selected Studies* (Addison-Wesley Series in Economics; Reading, Mass.: Addison-Wesley Publishing Company, 1978), p. vii.

2. Financial Accounting Standards Board, *Statement of Financial Accounting Standards No. 8*, "Accounting for the Translation of Foreign Currency Transactions and Foreign Currency Financial Statements" (Stamford, Conn.: FASB, 1975), par. 30.

3. Elwood L. Miller, *Accounting Problems of Multinational Enterprises* (Lexington, Mass.: Lexington Books, 1979), pp. 136-37.

4. Ibid., p. 138.

5. Ibid., p. 128.

6. Ibid., p. 127.

7. Ibid., pp. 127-28.

8. Ibid., p. 132.

9. Alan Teck, "International Business Under Floating Rates," *Columbia Journal of World Business* 11 (Fall, 1976), p. 61.

10. Frenkel and Johnson, *The Economics of Exchange Rates*, p. vii.

11. Miller, *Accounting Problems of Multinational Enterprises*, p. 138.

12. John E. Rule, "The Practical Business Effect of Exchange-rate Fluctuations," *Arthur Anderson Chronicle* 37 (September, 1977), p. 66.

13. Brian Kettell, "Foreign Exchange Exposure," *Accountancy* (England) 89 (March, 1978), p. 89.

14. Frenkel and Johnson, *The Economics of Exchange Rates*, p. 3.

15. "Stateless Money," *Business Week*, August 21, 1978, p. 80.

16. Frenkel and Johnson, *The Economics of Exchange Rates*, p. 29.

17. Ibid.

18. Ibid.

19. Ibid., pp. 1–25, 47–65.

20. Miller, *Accounting Problems of Multinational Enterprises*, p. 141.

Chapter 3

1. Financial Accounting Standards Board, *Statement of Financial Accounting Standards No. 52*, "Foreign Currency Translation" (Stamford, Conn.: FASB, 1981), par. 4.

2. Eldon S. Hendricksen, *Accounting Theory*, 3d ed. (Homewood, Ill.: Richard D. Irwin, Inc., 1977), pp. 35–37.

3. Robert L. McKinnell, "The FASB and Its Role in the Development of Accounting Principles in the United States," *Cost and Management* (May-June, 1975), p. 51.

4. Miller, *Accounting Problems of Multinational Enterprises*, pp. 145–48.

5. American Institute of Accountants, *AIA Year Book* (New York: AIA, 1932), pp. 237–40.

6. Miller, *Accounting Problems of Multinational Enterprises*, p. 149.

7. Ibid.

8. Ibid.

9. Samuel R. Hepworth, *Reporting Foreign Operations* (Ann Arbor, Mich.: University of Michigan, 1956).

10. National Association of Accountants, *Research Report No. 36*, "Management Accounting Problems in Foreign Operations" (New York: NAA, 1960).

11. Accounting Principles Board, Accounting Principles Board Opinion No. 6, "Status of Accounting Research Bulletins" (New York: AICPA, 1965), par. 18.

12. Accounting Principles Board, *Exposure Draft*, "Translating Foreign Operations" (New York: AICPA, 1971).

13. FASB, *Statement No. 8*, par. 2.

14. Ibid.

15. Miller, *Accounting Problems of Multinational Enterprises*, p. 151.

16. FASB, *Statement No. 8*, par. 6.

17. FASB, *Statement No. 52*, par. 150.

18. Ibid., par 2.

19. Ibid., par. 4.

20. Ibid., par. 5.

21. Ibid., par. 11.

22. Ibid., par. 10.

23. Ibid.

24. Ibid., par. 15.

Chapter 4

1. Philip E. Meyer, "Accounting Theory and Practice; Accounting for Foreign Currency," *Massachusetts CPA Review* (March/April, 1976), p. 37.

2. Raymond J. Clay, Jr. and William W. Holder, "A Guide to the Translation of Foreign Activities," *The National Public Accountant* (July, 1976), pp. 8–11.

3. John Y. Gray, "Translating Foreign Currency Transactions and Financial Statements," *The CPA Journal* (June, 1977), pp. 31–36.

4. Ibid., p. 36.

5. Ibid.

6. Clyde P. Stickney and Harold E. Wyman, "Coping with FASB No. 8," *The Accounting Forum* (Dec., 1977), p. 48.

7. Ibid.

8. Ibid., p. 50.

9. Ibid., p. 51.

10. Ibid., p. 52.

11. Ibid.

12. Ibid.

13. Marvin M. Deupree, "Is FASB #8 the Best Approach?" *Financial Executive* (January, 1978), p. 24.

14. Ibid., p. 26.

15. Ibid., p. 25.

16. "A Major Audit for FASB-8," *Business Week*, January 29, 1979, p. 102.

17. Ibid., p. 106.

18. Ibid.

19. Gerald I. White, "Review of FASB Statement No. 8," *Financial Analysts Journal* (March/April 1979), pp. 20–21, 79–80.

20. Ibid.

21. Marvin N. Schmitz, "Taxation of Foreign Exchange Gains and Losses," *Management Accounting* (July, 1976), pp. 49–51.

22. Michael L. Moore and John L. Kramer, "Tax and Accounting Rules for Currency Translation," *International Tax Journal* (Feb., 1977), pp. 238–73.

23. Ibid., p. 238.

24. "The 'New Reality,' " *Forbes*, June 15, 1976, pp. 37–40.

25. Ibid., p. 37.

26. Ibid.

27. Ibid.

28. Ibid.

29. Ibid., p. 40.

30. M.S. Forbes, "Why Can't Accountants be Practical?" *Forbes*, June 12, 1978, p. 28.

31. Ibid.

32. Ibid.

33. William D. Serfass, Jr., "Possible Undesirable Effects of FASB No. 8," *The CPA Journal* (May, 1976), p. 59.

34. Ibid.

35. Ibid.

36. Ibid., p. 60.

37. E.M. de Windt, "The New Rules on Financial Reporting — 'Who's on First — What's on Second'?" *Financial Executive* (December, 1976), p. 19.

38. Ibid.

39. Rita M. Rodriguez, "FASB No. 8: What Has it Done for Us?" *Financial Analyst Journal* (March/April, 1977), p. 41.

40. Ibid., p. 47.

41. William J. Bruns, "FASB 8: What Did it Really Do?" *The Accounting Forum* (December, 1977), p. 1.

42. Miller, *Accounting Problems of Multinational Enterprises*, p. 155.

43. Bruns, "FASB 8: What Did it Really Do?" p. 1.

44. Murray J. Bryant and John K. Shank, "Foreign Currency Accounting and FASB No. 8: Questioning the Economic Impact," *The Accounting Forum* (December, 1977), p. 14.

45. Ibid., p. 15.

46. Kerry Cooper, Donald R. Fraser, and R. Malcomb Richards, "The Impact of SFAS #8 on Financial Management Practices," *Financial Executive* (June, 1978), pp. 26–31.

47. Ibid., p. 26.

48. Ibid.

49. Ibid., p. 31.

50. Ibid.

51. Marjorie Stanley and Stanley B. Block, "Accounting and Economic Aspects of SFAS No. 8," *The International Journal of Accounting* (Spring, 1979), p. 149.

52. Ibid.

53. Ibid.

54. John K. Shank, Jesse F. Dillard, and Richard J. Murdock, "FASB No. 8 and the Decision Makers," *Financial Executive* (Feb., 1980), pp. 19–21.

55. Ibid.

56. Ibid., p. 23.

57. Ibid.

58. Philip M.J. Reckers and Martin E. Taylor, "FAS No. 8 – Does It Distort Financial Statements?" *The CPA Journal* (August, 1978), p. 34.

59. Ibid.

60. Leopold A. Bernstein, "The New Accounting for Foreign Currency Transactions – Some Implications for Financial Analysis," *Journal of Commercial Bank Lending* (October, 1976), pp. 59-63.

61. Ibid.

62. William C. Norby, "Accounting for Financial Analysis," *Financial Analysts Journal* (Sept./Oct., 1978), p. 20.

63. "Banks Cash in on FASB-8," *Business Week*, December 6, 1976, p. 104.

64. "A Corporate Scheme for Currency Swapping," *Business Week*, September 5, 1977, p. 70.

65. Alan Teck, "Beyond FAS No. 8: Defining Other Exposures," *Management Accounting* (December, 1978), p. 57.

66. Paul Munter, "Currency Strategies Under FASB 8: An Empirical Analysis," *International Tax Journal* (December, 1979), pp. 85-95.

67. James T. Sherwin, "Foreign Exchange Exposure Management," *Financial Executive* (May, 1979), p. 18.

68. Ibid.

69. Gaffney Feskoe, "Reducing Currency Risk in a Volatile Foreign Exchange Market," *Management Accounting* (September, 1980), p. 24.

70. "U.S. FASB Selects Current Rate Translation Method, Surprising Disposition of Adjustments," *Business International Money Report*, March 28, 1980.

71. Arlene Hershman, "Hate FASB 8? You Find a Substitute," *Dun's Review*, February 1981, p. 76.

72. Ibid., p. 78

73. Ibid.

74. Ibid.

75. Ibid.

76. Ibid.

77. "U.S. FASB Selects Current Rate Translation Method, Surprising Disposition of Adjustments," p. 103.

78. "MAP on Foreign Currency Translation," *Management Accounting* (November, 1981), p. 8.

79. "U.S. FASB Selects Current Rate Translation Method, Surprising Disposition of Adjustments," p. 103.

80. "Once More with Feeling," *Forbes*, October 13, 1980, pp. 192-94.

81. Norlin G. Rueschhoff and Leonard M. Savoie, "Improved Accounting Methods for Foreign Currency Translation," *Financial Executive* (February, 1982), pp. 35–42.

82. Ibid.

83. David J. Duane, "Accounting for Foreign Currency FASB 52," *Valueline: Selection and Opinion*, December 25, 1981, p. 320.

84. "SFAS No. 52 Behind the Scenes: Review of the New Foreign Currency Rules," *WG&L Accounting News* (April, 1982), p. 2.

85. Ibid., p. 23.

86. Joseph E. Connor, "Accounting for the Upward Float in Foreign Currencies," *The Journal of Accounting* (June, 1972), p. 43.

87. Ibid.

88. Lee J. Seidler, "An Income Approach to Financial Statements," *The CPA Journal* (January, 1972), p. 31.

89. Ibid., p. 32.

90. Ibid., p. 34.

91. Edgar M. Barrett and Leslie L. Spero, "Accounting Determinants of Foreign Exchange Gains and Losses," *Financial Analysts Journal* (March/April, 1975), p. 26.

92. John K. Shank, "FASB Statement 8 Resolved Foreign Currency Accounting—Or Did It?" *Financial Analysts Journal* (July/August, 1976), p. 55.

93. Ibid., pp. 57–60.

94. Thomas G. Evans, "Some Concerns About Exposure After the FASB's Statement No. 8," *Financial Executive* (November, 1976), p. 30.

95. Ibid., pp. 28–30.

96. Ronald M. Copeland and Robert W. Ingram, "An Evaluation of Accounting Alternatives for Foreign Currency Transactions," *The International Journal of Accounting* (Spring, 1978), p. 26.

97. Ibid., pp. 15–26.

98. John K. Shank and Gary S. Shamis, "Reporting Foreign Currency Adjustments: A Disclosure Perspective," *The Journal of Accountancy* (April, 1979), p. 59.

99. Ibid., p. 64.

100. Ibid.

101. Ibid., pp. 59–64.

102. Paul Kolton, "FASB in the 1980s: Standard Setting in a Changing Environment," *The Journal of Accountancy* (March, 1982), pp. 84–92.

Chapter 5

1. General Motors Corporation, 1981 Annual Report, p. 20.

2. Honeywell Incorporated, 1981 Annual Report, p. 33.

3. RCA, 1981 Annual Report, p. 43.

4. Ibid.

5. Mobil Corporation, 1981 Annual Report, p. 20.

6. Ibid., p. 37.

7. American Express Company, 1981 Annual Report, p. 70.

8. Ibid., p. 75.

9. International Business Machines, 1981 Annual Report, p. 23.

10. Ibid.

11. Ibid.

12. Ibid.

13. Ibid.

14. Ibid., p. 25.

15. Ibid., p. 25.

16. Ibid., p. 25.

17. Ibid., p. 29.

18. Ibid., p. 30.

19. Avon Products, Incorporated, 1981 Annual Report, p. 34.

20. Ibid.

21. Ibid., p. 35.

22. Ibid.

23. Ibid.

24. Ibid.

25. Ibid., p. 46

26. Shank and Shamis, "Reporting Foreign Currency Adjustments: A Disclosure Perspective," pp. 59–65.

27. Norby, "Accounting for Financial Analysis," p. 20.

Chapter 6

1. Shank and Shamis, "Reporting Foreign Currency Adjustments: A Disclosure Perspective," pp. 59–65.

2. Herbert E. Phillips and John C. Ritchie, *Investment Analysis and Portfolio Selection* (Cincinnati, Ohio: South-Western Publishing Co., 1983), pp. 206-207.

3. Shank and Shamis, "Reporting Foreign Currency Adjustments: A Disclosure Perspective," pp. 59–65.

4. Norby, "FASB Review Program," p. 20.

5. John J. Curran, "Making Economic Sense of Foreign Earnings," *Fortune*, November 2, 1981, pp. 157–160.

6. *Accounting Principles Board Opinion No. 15*, "Earnings per Share" (New York: AICPA, 1969), par. 1–2.

Chapter 7

1. Miller, *Accounting Problems of Multinational Enterprises*, pp. 140–41, 160.

2. Ibid., p. 160.

3. James A. Schweikart, "We Must End Consolidation of Foreign Subsidiaries," *Management Accounting* (August, 1981), pp. 15–18.

4. FASB, *Statement of Financial Accounting Concepts No. 1*, par. 34.

5. Ibid., par. 37.

6. Ibid., par. 40.

7. Ibid., par. 43.

8. Ibid., par. 47.

9. Ibid., par. 50.

10. Ibid., par. 54.

Bibliography

Books

Arpas, Jeffery S., and Lee H. Radebaugh. *International Accounting and Multinational Enterprises*. Boston: Warren, Gorham and Lamont, 1981.

Frenkel, Jacob A., and Harry G. Johnson, eds. *The Economic of Exchange Rates*. Reading, Mass.: Addison-Wesley, 1978.

Hendricksen, Eldon S. *Accounting Theory*. 3d ed. Homewood, Ill.: Richard D. Irwin, Inc., 1977.

Hepworth, Samuel R. *Reporting Foreign Operations*. Ann Arbor, Mich.: University of Michigan, 1956.

Miller, Elwood L. *Accounting Problems of Multinational Enterprises*. Lexington, Mass.: D.C. Heath and Company, 1979.

Phillips, Herbert E., and John C. Ritchie. *Investment Analysis and Portfolio Selection*. Cincinnati, Ohio: South-Western Publishing Co., 1983.

Watt, George C., Richard M. Hammer and Marianne Burge. *Accounting for the Multinational Corporation*. Homewood, Ill.: Dow Jones-Irwin, 1978.

Articles

Adkins, Lynn. "New Management Headache." *Dunn's Review* 110 (October, 1977): 72–77.

Aggarwal, Raj. "Highlights on FASB-8." *Business Week*, March 5, 1979, p. 11.

Ankrom, Robert K. "Top Level Approach to the Foreign Exchange Problem." *Harvard Business Review* 52 (July-August, 1974): 79–80.

"BAI Issues Accounting Bulletin on Foreign Currency Transactions" (News report). *Journal of Accountancy* 143 (February, 1977): 20–22.

"Banks Cash in on FASB-8" (International money management). *Business Week*, December 6, 1976, pp. 104, 107.

Barrett, M. Edgar, and Leslie L. Spero. "Accounting Determinants of Foreign Exchange Gains and Losses." *Financial Analysts Journal* 31 (March/April, 1975): 26–30.

Bent, Barbara. "How FASB-8 Should be Changed," (Corporate financing). *Institutional Investor* 12 (November, 1978): 73–74, 79.

Beresford, Dennis R., and Robert D. Neary. "FASB Expects to Amend Statement No. 8." *Financial Executive*, April 1979.

_____, and Robert D. Neary. "FASB Slates Major Changes to Statement No. 8" (Financial reporting briefs). *Financial Executive* 47 (September, 1979): 11.

_____, and Robert D. Neary. "FASB Tries Again on Foreign Currency Translation." *Financial Executive*, August 1981.

Bernstein, Leopold A. "New Accounting for Foreign Currency Transactions——Some Implications for Financial Analysis." *Journal of Commercial Bank Lending* 59 (October, 1976): 59–63.

Bhushan, Bhuwan. "Effects of Inflation and Currency Fluctuation." *Management Accounting* (NAA) 56 (July, 1974): 17–19.

Bisgay, Louis, ed. "FASB Proposes Overhaul of FAS No. 8." *Management Accounting*, November 1980.

———, ed. "MAP on Foreign Currency Translation." *Management Accounting*, February 1981.

———, ed. "MAP on Foreign Currency Translation." *Management Accounting*, November 1981.

———, ed. "New Rules Proposed on Foreign Currency Issue." *Management Accounting*, September 1981.

———, ed. "Tentative Conclusions on FAS No. 8." *Management Accounting*, June 1980.

Bruns, William J. "FASB 8: What Did it Really Do?" *Accounting Forum* 47 (December, 1977): 1–10.

Bryant, Murray J., and Mary Claire Mahaney. "The Politics of Standard Setting." *Management Accounting*, March 1981.

Burton, John C. "Emerging Trends in Financial Reporting." *Journal of Accountancy*, July 1981.

Carstairs, Ralph. "Accounting and Management Aspects of Foreign Exchange Transactions." *Australian Accountant* 49 (August 1979): 454–60, 463–64, 493.

Clay, Raymond J., and William W. Holder. "Guide to the Translation of Foreign Activities." *National Public Accountant* 21 (July 1976): 8–11.

Connor, Joseph E. "Accounting Reality," (Statement in quotes). *Journal of Accountancy* 147 (February 1979): 78–80.

———. "Accounting Reality." Address before the Columbia Business School Club of New York. New York: Price, Waterhouse & Co., C1978, 8p. 111.1C.

———. "Putting Accounting Developments in Perspective." *Financial Executive* 42 (May, 1974): 74–78, 80.

Cooper, Kerry, Donald R. Fraser and R. Malcolm Richards. "Management Practices." *Financial Executive* 46 (June, 1978): 26–31.

Copeland, Ronald, and Robert W. Ingram. "An Evaluation of Accounting Alternatives for Foreign Currency Transactions." *International Journal of Accounting* 13 (Spring, 1978): 15–26.

"A Corporate Scheme for Currency Swapping." *Business Week*, September 5, 1977, p. 70.

Curran, John J. "Making Economic Sense of Foreign Earnings." *Fortune*, November 2, 1981.

de Windt, E.M. "Opinion: The New Rules on Financial Reporting—Who's on First? What's on Second?" *Financial Executive* 44 (December, 1976): 18–23.

Deupree, Marvin M. "FASB No. 8 The Best Approach?" *Financial Executive* 46 (January, 1978): 24–29.

Dieteman, Gerald J. "Evaluating Multinational Performance Under FAS No. 8." *Management Accounting*, May, 1980.

Duane, David J. "Accounting for Foreign Currency FASB 52." *Valueline: Selection and Opinion*, December 25, 1981.

Duangploy, Orapin. "Sensitivity of Earnings Per Share to Different Foreign Currency Translation Methods." *International Journal of Accounting Education and Research* 14 (Spring 1979): 121–34.

Earl, Michael, and Dean Parson. "Value Accounting for Currency Translations." *Accounting and Business Research* (England) 30 (Spring, 1978): 92–100.

"Eurosterling Haven for the Multinationals" (International money management). *Business Week*, March 13, 1978: 81–82.

Evans, Thomas G. "Diversity in Foreign Currency Translation Methods — A Proposal for Uniformity." *CPA Journal* 44 (February, 1974): 41–45.

_____. "Foreign Currency Translation Practices Abroad." *CPA Journal* 44 (June 1974): 47–50.

_____. "Some Concerns About Exposure After the FASB's Statement No. 8." *Financial Executive* 44 (November, 1976): 28–30.

Fantl, Irving L. "Problems with Currency Translation — A Report on FASB No. 8." *Financial Executive* 47 (December, 1979): 33–36.

"FASB 8 Versus the Real World (Faces Behind the Figures)." *Forbes* 122 (July 24, 1978): 86.

Feskoe, Gaffney. "Reducing Currency Risks in a Volatile Foreign Exchange Market." *Management Accounting*, September 1980.

"Floating Earnings (Statistical Spotlight)." *Forbes* 122 (September 4, 1978): 87.

Forbes, Malcolm S. "Why Can't Accountants be Practical? Facts and Comments." *Forbes* 121 (June 12, 1978): 23.

"Foreign Exchange: Why the Float Gets Dirtier." *Business Week*, November 22, 1976.

Fredrikson, E. Bruce. "Financial Analyst (and Academic) Views FASB 8." *Accounting Forum* 47 (December, 1977): 31–44.

_____. "Valuation of Noncurrent Foreign Currency Monetary Claims." *International Journal of Accounting Education and Research* 9 (Fall, 1973): 149–58.

Frey, Karen M. "Management of Foreign Exchange Risk with Forward Contracts." *Management Accounting* (NAA) 58 (March, 1977): 45–48.

Gray, John Y. "Translating Foreign Currency Transactions and Financial Statements." *CPA Journal* 47 (June, 1977): 31–36.

_____. "Translating Foreign Exchange Risk with Forward Contracts." *Management Accounting* (NAA) 58 (March, 1977): 45–48.

Greene, Richard. "Once More with Feeling." *Forbes*, October, 13, 1980.

Griffin, Paul A. "What Harm Has FASB 8 Actually Done?" *Harvard Business Review* 57 (July-August, 1979): 8, 12, 14, 18.

Hekman, Christine R. "On Revising FASB 8 — Use a Band-aid or Major Surgery?" *Harvard Business Review*, May-June 1980.

Hershman, Arlene. "Hate FASB 8? You Find a Substitute." *Dunn's Review*, February 1981.

Horwitz, Bertrand, and Kolodny, Richard. "Has the FASB Hurt Small High-technology Companies?" *Harvard Business Review*, May-June 1980.

Hunter, Robert L., Gary M. Cunningham, and Thomas G. Evans. "Are Multinational Liquidity Models Worth Their Cost?" *Management Accounting* (NAA) 61 (December, 1979): 51–56.

Kettell, Brian. "Foreign Exchange Exposure." *Accountancy* (England) 89 (March, 1978): 83–84, 86, 89.

Kolton, Paul. "FASB in the 1980s: Standard Setting in a Changing Environment." *The Journal of Accountancy* 153 (March, 1982).

Leak, David K. "LIFO: A Good Marriage with FASB 8 for Multinationals." *Financial Executive* 45 (February, 1977): 38–39.

Macinthosh, John. "Accounting for Gain or Losses on Foreign Exchange Transactions." *South Africa Chartered Accountant* 13 (September, 1977): 311–13.

McKinnell, Robert L. "The FASB and Its Role in the Development of Accounting Principles in the United States." *Cost and Management*, May-June, 1975.

McMonnies, Peter N., and Bryan J. Rankin. "Accounting for Foreign Currency Translation." *Accountant's Magazine* (Scotland) 81 (June, 1977): 241–43.

"A Major Audit for FASB-8" (Accounting). *Business Week*, January 29, 1979, pp. 102, 106.

Mathur, Ike. "Attitudes of Financial Executives Toward Foreign Exchange Issues." *Financial Executive*, October, 1980.

———, and David Loy. "Foreign Currency Translation: Survey of Corporate Treasurers." *Management Accounting*, September 1981.

Merjos, Anna. "Lost in Translation, the Effects of FASB-8 Are Rippling Far and Wide." *Barron's*, December 6, 1976: 11, 24–26.

Meyer, Philip E. "Accounting for Foreign Currency" (Accounting Theory & Practice). *Massachusetts CPA Review* 50 (March/April, 1976): 37.

Miller, Paul B.W. "New View on Comparability." *Journal of Accountancy* 146 (August, 1978): 70–77.

Minard, Lawrence. "So Waddya Suggest?" (Numbers Game). *Forbes* 122 (November 13, 1978): 78–83.

Moore, Michael L., and John L. Kramer. "Tax and Accounting Rules for Currency Translation." *International Tax Journal* 3 (February, 1977): 238–73.

Munter, Paul. "Currency Strategies Under FASB 8: An Empirical Analysis." *International Tax Journal* 6 (December, 1979): 85–95.

"The New Reality—FASB Statement 8" (Numbers Game). *Forbes* 117 (June 15, 1976): 37, 40.

"Nightmare of FASB-8," (Numbers Game). *Forbes* 122 (September 18, 1978): 187–88.

Norby, William C. "FASB Review Program," (Accounting for Financial Analysis). *Financial Analysts Journal* 34 (September/October, 1978): 18–20.

Norr, David. "Currency Translation and the Analyst." *Financial Analyst Journal* 32 (July/August, 1976): 46–54.

———. "Foreign Exchange and Disclosure." *Accounting Forum* 47 (December, 1977): 63–75.

———. "Improved Foreign Exchange Disclosure for the Investor," (Accounting for financial analysis). *Financial Analysts Journal* 33 (March/April 1977): 17–20.

Pakkala, A.L. "Foreign Exchange Accounting of Multinational Corporations." *Financial Analysts Journal* 31 (March/April, 1975): 32–34, 36, 38–41, 76.

Piper, Andrew. "Accounting for Overseas Currencies." *International Journal of Accounting Education and Research* 12 (Fall, 1976): 63–90.

Pleak, Ruth E. "Analysis of FASB's Treatment of Foreign Currency Translation." *Management Accounting* 59 (September, 1977): 29–32.

Polk, Raemon. "Financial and Tax Aspects of Planning for Foreign Currency Exchange Rate Fluctuations." *Taxes—The Tax Magazine* 56 (March, 1978): 159–68.

Ravenscroft, Donald P. "Translating Foreign Currency Under U.S. Tax Laws." *Financial Executive* 42 (September, 1974): 58–60, 62–64, 66–69.

Reckers, Philip M.J., and Martin E. Taylor. "FASB No. 8—Does It Distort Financial Statements." *CPA Journal* 48 (August, 1978): 31–34. 察 33.32

Rodrigues, Rita M. "FASB No. 8. What Has It Done for Us?" *Financial Analyst Journal* 33 (March/April, 1977): 40–47.

Roof, Bradley M. "FASB No. 8—Did It Help or Hinder Multinational Reporting?" *Financial Executive*, March, 1982.

Rosenfield, Paul. "Accounting for Foreign Branches and Subsidiaries." *International Journal of Accounting Education and Research* 7 (Spring, 1972): 35–44.

Rueschhoff, Norlin G., and Savoie, Leonard M. "Improved Accounting Methods for Foreign Currency Translation." *Financial Executive*, February, 1982.

Rule, John E. "Practical Business Effect of Exchange Rate Fluctuations." *Arthur Andersen Chronicle* 37 (September 1977): 63–75.

Schmitz, Marvin N. "Taxation of Foreign Exchange Gains and Losses." *Management Accounting*, July, 1976.

Schweikart, James A. "We Must End Consolidation of Foreign Subsidiaries." *Management Accounting*, August, 1981, pp. 15–18.

Seidler, Lee J. "An Income Approach to Financial Statements." *The CPA Journal*, January, 1972.

Serfass, William D. "Possible Undesirable Effects of FASB No. 8" (Auditing and Reporting). *CPA Journal* 46 (May, 1976): 59–60.

"SFAS No. 52 Behind the Scenes: Review of the New Foreign Currency Rules." *WG & L Accounting News*, April, 1982.

Shank, John K. "FASB Statement 8 Resolved Foreign Currency Accounting – or Did it?" *Financial Analyst Journal* 32 (July/August, 1976): 55–61.

————, and Murray J. Bryant. "Foreign Currency Accounting and FASB No. 8: Questioning the Economic Impact." *Accounting Forum* 47 (December, 1977): 11–29.

————, Jesse F. Dillard, and Richard J. Murdock. "FASB No. 8 and the Decision-Makers." *Financial Executive*, February, 1980.

————, and Gary S. Shamis. "Reporting Foreign Currency Adjustments: A Disclosure Perspective." *Journal of Accountancy* 147 (April, 1979): 59–65.

Sherwin, James T. "Foreign Exchange Exposure Management." *Financial Executive* 47 (May, 1979): 18–23.

Shwayder, Keith R. "Consistency Between Price Level Accounting and Foreign Exchange Accounting." *Accounting Forum* 47 (December, 1977): 77–93.

Smith, John L. "Improving Reported Earnings." *Management Accounting*, September 1981.

Stanley, Marjorie R., and Stanley B. Block. "Accounting and Economic Aspects of FASB No. 8." *International Journal of Accounting Education and Research* 14 (Spring, 1979): 135–55.

Stickney, Clyde P., and Harold E. Wyman. "Coping with FASB Statement No. 8." *Accounting Forum* 47 (December, 1977): 45–61.

"Studies Issued on Effects of FASB No. 8." *Journal of Accountancy* 147 (March, 1979): 22.

"Survey Finds Many Corporate Execs. Favor Foreign Exchange Rule Repeal" (News report). *Journal of Accountancy* 146 (August, 1978): 26, 28, 30.

Teck, Alan. "Beyond FASB No. 8: Defining Other Exposures." *Management Accounting* (NAA) 60 (December, 1978): 54–57.

————. "International Business Under Floating Rates." *Columbia Journal of World Business* 11 (Fall, 1976): 60–71.

"U.S. FASB Selects Current Rate Translation Method, Surprising Disposition of Adjustments." *Business International Money Report*, March 28, 1980.

"Ways Out of the Currency Translation Mess," (Accounting). *Business Week*, August 6, 1979: 80.

Weberman, Ben "New Dollar Diplomacy." *Forbes* 121 (January 23, 1978): 39–42.

White, Gerald I. "Review of FASB No. 8," (Accounting for Financial Analysis). *Financial Analysts Journal* 35 (March/April, 1979): 20–21, 79–80.

Willey, Russell W. "In Defense of FASB No. 8." *Management Accounting* (NAA) 61 (December, 1979): 36–40.

Official Reports

Accounting Principles Board. *Accounting Principles Board Opinion No. 6*, "Status of Accounting Research Bulletins." New York: American Institute of Certified Public Accountants, 1965.

Accounting Principles Board. *Exposure Draft*, "Translating Foreign Operations." New York: American Institute of Certified Public Accountants, 1971.

Accounting Principles Board Opinion No. 15, "Earnings per Share." New York: American Institute of Certified Public Accountants, 1969.

Financial Accounting Standards Board. *Statement of Financial Accounting Concepts No. 1*, "Objectives of Financial Reporting by Business Enterprises." Stamford, Conn.: FASB, November 1978.

Financial Accounting Standards Board. *Statement of Financial Accounting Standards No. 8*, "Accounting for the Translation of Foreign Currency Transactions and Foreign Currency Financial Statements." Stamford, Conn.: FASB, 1975.

Financial Accounting Standards Board. *Statement of Financial Accounting Standards No. 52*, "Foreign Currency Translation." Stamford, Conn.: FASB, 1981.

National Association of Accountants. Research Report No. 36, "Management Accounting Problems in Foreign Operations." New York: National Association of Accountants, 1960.

Annual Reports

American Express Company. 1981 Annual Report.
Avon Products, Incorporated. 1981 Annual Report.
General Motors Corporation. 1981 Annual Report.
Honeywell Incorporated. 1981 Annual Report.
International Business Machines. 1981 Annual Report.
Mobil Corporation. 1981 Annual Report.
RCA. 1981 Annual Report.

Index